# A PEAKBAGGER'S GUIDE TO THE CANADIAN ROCKIES: NORTH

# A PEAKBAGGER'S GUIDE TO THE CANADIAN ROCKIES: NORTH

Ben Nearingburg

*and*

Eric Coulthard

**RMB**

RMB | Rocky Mountain Books Ltd.
rmbooks.com   @rmbooks   facebook.com/rmbooks

Cataloguing data available from Library and Archives Canada
ISBN 978-1-77160-198-6 (softcover)
· ISBN 978-1-77160-199-3 (electronic)

All photos are by Ben Nearingburg unless otherwise noted.
Cover design: Chyla Cardinal
Layout design: Lin Oosterhoff

Printed and bound in Canada by Friesens

Distributed in Canada by Heritage Group Distribution and in the U.S. by Publishers Group West

For information on purchasing bulk quantities of this book, or to obtain media excerpts or invite the author to speak at an event, please visit rmbooks.com and select the "Contact Us" tab.

RMB | Rocky Mountain Books is dedicated to the environment and committed to reducing the destruction of old-growth forests. Our books are produced with respect for the future and consideration for the past.

We acknowledge the financial support of the Government of Canada through the Canada Book Fund and the Canada Council for the Arts, and of the province of British Columbia through the British Columbia Arts Council and the Book Publishing Tax Credit.

**Disclaimer**

The actions described in this book may be considered inherently dangerous activities. Individuals undertake these activities at their own risk. The information put forth in this guide has been collected from a variety of sources and is not guaranteed to be completely accurate or reliable. Many conditions and some information may change owing to weather and numerous other factors beyond the control of the authors and publishers. Individuals or groups must determine the risks, use their own judgment, and take full responsibility for their actions. Do not depend on any information found in this book for your own personal safety. Your safety depends on your own good judgment based on your skills, education, and experience.

It is up to the users of this guidebook to acquire the necessary skills for safe experiences and to exercise caution in potentially hazardous areas. The authors and publishers of this guide accept no responsibility for your actions or the results that occur from another's actions, choices, or judgments. If you have any doubt as to your safety or your ability to attempt anything described in this guidebook, do not attempt it.

# CONTENTS

Preface..................................................................................6

Acknowledgements.......................................................7

Introduction...........................................................8

## ROUTE AREAS

Yellowhead Highway East.....................................25

Snaring and Celestine Lake roads........................54

Yellowhead Highway West....................................71

Maligne Lake.........................................................103

Tonquin Valley......................................................131

Icefields Parkway..................................................155

Le Grand Brazeau..................................................197

South Boundary Trail and Whitehorse Wildland Provincial Park..................219

Mount Robson Provincial Park.............................233

Valemount..............................................................263


Bibliography..........................................................278

Useful contacts......................................................280

Table of Winter Peaks...........................................281

Index of All Peaks and Routes..............................282

# PREFACE

The idea for this guidebook came together when the authors were planning a weekend peakbagging trip with friends. The conversation went kind of like the following: "Why not head to Jasper?" "Jasper?! There's nothing to climb in Jasper. Let's go to Banff instead."

Hopefully after reading this book you will agree there are certainly plenty of excellent objectives to ascend, not only in Jasper National Park but also the surrounding provincial parks and wilderness areas. As a "peakbagger's guide" this book contains a variety of different types of routes, from hikes, to scrambles, to alpine climbs and ski tours. As such, this book caters to many folks with different interests, so be sure to read the Difficulty Ratings section to be aware of the requirements and classifications each type of trip entails before heading out!

It is our hope that this book will inspire you to get out and explore the wondrous wilds that the Canadian Rockies provide and spend a little time off the beaten trail.

Have fun out there,

Ben and Eric

# ACKNOWLEDGEMENTS

This book is the result of a great deal of effort by a large number of people. Specifically, the authors would like to thank Steven Song and Vern Dewit for providing images and great company along the majority of the routes described here. Additional images were provided by Mike Mitchell and David P. Jones. Their contributions are greatly appreciated. We would also like to thank Ken Harris for his considerable help with editing the text (tracking down rogue semicolons is often a thankless but essential task). While all of the routes described in this book are based on personal experience from our trips, many of the historical facts and relevant details have been collected from other references. First and foremost of those was *Canadian Mountain Place Names*, by Glen W. Boles, Roger W. Laurilla and William L. Putnam, which is quite possibly the most complete compendium of Rockies name lore in existence. Some further information was researched from the seminal *Handbook of the Canadian Rockies*, by Ben Gadd. Elevation data was obtained from a variety of sources that have been averaged on summitsearch.org.

# INTRODUCTION

## WHAT IS PEAKBAGGING?

The key contributors to the book (left to right): Steven Song, Ben Nearingburg, Eric Coulthard and Vern Dewit on the summit of Mount Prince George.

To many who pick up this book, "peakbagging" may sound like a very unfamiliar term. Peakbagging can be loosely defined as "collecting summits," and it has become a popular pastime for grizzled mountaineers and energetic weekend warriors alike. As with collecting rare coins or hockey cards, much of the value of peakbagging is internal to the collector. In Ben and Eric's experience, the memories obtained during the ascents are much more rewarding than the summits themselves, but it is hard not to smile when reaching the summit of a remote peak and casting your gaze out over a pristine mountain vista. Compared to a dedicated sport climber, hiker or alpinist, the modern peakbagger is a creature of many trades. Some peaks are best climbed by scrambling up scree slopes (a very common form of ascent in the rubbly Rockies), some require steep technical rock, and others are best tackled on skis or snowshoes, while winter-mellowed creeks and rivers allow for better access. As such, many of the routes described here are recommended for multiple seasons (with seasonal route variations described). Routes that are recommended for winter also have ATES ratings giving an approximation of the avalanche hazard on the described line. Pay careful attention to the Safety, Difficulty Ratings, Approaches and Equipment sections in the book and always ask a more experienced mountaineer if uncertain of any terms or techniques.

# SAFETY

Mountains can be dangerous places and the Canadian Rockies are no exception. There are quite a few hazard to be aware of before setting out on the routes described here (or on an adventure of any sort). This section is an introduction to possible safety hazards you might encounter, but it is far from a valid substitute for formal training in mountain safety. It is highly recommended that you take an ACMG (Association of Canadian Mountain Guides) or UIAA (Union internationale des associations d'alpinisme / International Climbing and Mountaineering Federation) approved course from an ACMG guide when you are first moving into self-guided pursuits in the hills.

## ON LIFE AND DEATH IN THE MOUNTAINS: THE FINE LINE BETWEEN CALM AND CALAMITY

When starting out on a mountain trek, spirits are often high, with limitless enthusiasm propelling a budding peakbagger upward. It is easy to forget that one slip, one mistake, even on relatively tame terrain, could very easily turn into a **fatal** event. Despite the casual attitude that many people and institutions take towards travel in the mountains (both backcountry and front country), it is a sobering truth that mountains can indeed be very dangerous. In the next few pages, several different types of hazards that peakbaggers in the Rockies will face are discussed. While this information can be helpful and should be reviewed before setting off on any of the routes described in this book, it is by no means a complete discussion. The safety of yourself and your fellow peakbaggers should be the first and most important priority of any trip! Unlike many places in the modern world, travel in the Canadian Rockies is usually remote and self-supported. If something goes wrong you cannot depend on a helicopter rescue crew to be dispatched and quickly whisk you away to safety. Rescues are complicated procedures, and weather or location, among other factors, can easily result in injured parties being stranded for many days. You must carry supplies and have the skills required to survive until help can arrive or you can return to civilization on your own. Any of the routes described in this book can result in injury or even death if mistakes are made. Thankfully, much of the hazard can be mitigated by keeping to a few general rules.

First, always remember to use common sense. If a particular route description suggests following a line that seems dangerous, **do not** follow it. Conditions in alpine routes can vary from year to year, and changing conditions can turn historically safe lines into perilous routes. While the authors have made every effort to make the route descriptions in this book accurate and up to date, trust your eyes and ears to evaluate current conditions.

Secondly, keep in mind that reaching a summit is only half the battle. It is often quoted that statistically more incidents in the mountains occur on descent rather than ascent. Stay mindful of factors such as changing weather, amount of daylight and personal fitness when evaluating progress on a trip, and turn back if anything doesn't feel right.

Lastly, there is no substitute for experience. While guidebooks and textbooks on mountain skills can be useful in laying the foundation for safe travel, only personal experience will make an experienced mountaineer. Learning from more seasoned climbers and hikers, participating in group events (such as with the Alpine Club of Canada) or hiring an ACMG-certified guide to build practical skills are all ways to enhance personal experience in lower-risk settings.

## TERRAIN

The areas described in this book contain a great variety of terrain, from open alpine meadows and vast scree and boulder slopes, to impressive icefields, to dense, swampy bogs. A peakbagger in the Rockies could experience all of these terrain features on one trip (possibly even in one day!). As a result, it is important to be aware of the different hazards you could encounter in each type of terrain. In individual route descriptions, additional equipment or hazards are identified, but you can safely assume a few constants for all of the areas in the book.

First, the Rockies are notorious for loose, chossy rock, and almost every route will have scree piles. One of the forefathers of modern technical climbing in the Rockies, David Cheesmond, famously said that "if you can climb here, you can climb anywhere," largely based on the objective hazards related to untrustworthy holds that climbers face in the Rockies. Thankfully for the peakbagger, the crumbling Rockies often allow for less-technical ascent lines on scree rather than monolithic faces as found in other ranges in the world. Conversely, though, scree can create both tricky footing and rockfall issues. Rockfall is a significant concern on almost all of the routes described in this book and can be triggered by both natural and artificial (i.e., human) causes and can cause injuries or even fatalities.

Second, several of the routes described here (specifically in the Le Grand Brazeau chapter) involve glacier crossings. Travelling on glaciers is inherently dangerous due to the presence of mazes of crevasses lurking beneath inviting snow slopes. Do not attempt any travel on glaciated terrain unless you have been trained in crevasse rescue techniques and are carrying appropriate equipment. If the sentence "I'll whip up a quick 6-to-1 and fish you out" doesn't mean anything to you, you should seek a specialized glacier rescue course before even considering setting out.

Third, some routes in the book require crossing flowing water (be it in rivers, creeks or the multitude of other terms people have derived for essentially the same phenomenon). Crossing rivers in the Rockies can often be the crux of a trip, especially in the spring when snowmelt causes waterways to swell to dangerous heights and perilous speeds. So of course individual route descriptions note the times when you can expect dangerous crossing conditions, but you should still **always use common sense before attempting any crossing**. Keep your pack loose and unbuckled so that if you do get swept away, your pack will not pull you down with it. If you expect a river crossing, it is a good idea to pack an extra pair of lightweight shoes (sandals or runners work well) rather than wading across barefoot.

Lastly, in addition to outstanding peaks, the Rockies are also home to some exceptionally heinous bushwhacking. Do not underestimate the physical and mental stress that bushwhacking can place on a peakbagging trip. The strain on morale alone if reduced to a 1 km per hour pace through a dense patch of krummholz or a fearsome copse of alders can turn a pleasant trip into a horrendous nightmare. Additionally, take great care when moving through bush, to avoid damaging the environment (and yourself).

## ANIMALS AND PLANTS

One of the great allures of the Rockies compared to many mountainous regions in the world is the quantity and diversity of animal and plant life regularly encountered. As Parks tells you with signs, pamphlets and other sources of information, do not feed the wildlife. Animals are able to survive best on their natural diets, and critters that become conditioned to human intervention often become dependent on people and will move out of their wild environments. The Rockies are home to many large beasts: black bears, grizzly bears, large cats, wolves, moose and caribou to name a few. If you encounter one of these critters in the wild, remember that they are often as afraid of you as you are of them, if not more so. Use common sense and don't startle or provoke animals; they will react according to the threat you present.

Bears deserve special mention. While attacks on humans by bears are rare, they do occur, and there are several measures you can take to reduce the chance of a dangerous encounter. Parks Canada recommends that hikers and mountaineers make noise, watch for fresh bear scat, avoid bringing dogs into the backcountry (they are expressly prohibited in many areas), travel in groups of at least four people, use official trails and only during daylight hours, and never approach an animal carcass. Some of these recommendations (such as only travelling on official trails) will not serve the peakbagger, but the thinking behind the guidelines is solid. Furthermore, carrying bear spray (a concentrated form of capsaicin) is advisable when going into the backcountry **provided you know how to use it effectively**. Consult the literature on bear awareness and bear safety available from Parks Canada to see current recommended practices. Occasionally Parks will post warnings or closures for areas due to the presence of bears; be sure to check with the visitor centre or the Parks website before heading out.

One of the other types of critter in the Rockies that deserves mentioning are ticks. Ticks are a yearly annoyance that come out in the spring as the mountains start to emerge from winter. As parasites, ticks like to hang on foliage (particularly along popular routes) and wait for a passerby to brush into them. It is often very difficult to feel a tick on your skin, as they secrete a mild anesthetic which masks their presence. After travelling through a bushy section (particularly if you are wearing shorts and a t-shirt), you should double-check yourself and your partners for ticks (from stem to stern; ticks particularly enjoy less accessible places such as under-clothing). Remove any you find, using a pair of tweezers. See a backcountry-oriented medical text or Alberta Health for current information on how to properly remove ticks. Ticks are known carriers of Rocky Mountain spotted fever and Lyme disease. If you are concerned about the possibility of an infection, save the tick in a plastic bag or other container and take it to a medical centre for analysis.

While there are many edible plants in the Rockies (especially berries), the authors do not advise consuming anything from the wild unless you are skilled at identifying local flora (books such as Ben Gadd's *Handbook of the Canadian Rockies* are a good starting point).

One particular plant that may vex peakbaggers in Mount Robson Provincial Park is devil's club, a broad, bushy shrub with many barbs coating its stem. If you happen to get pierced by a barb, remove it as quickly as you can, as it can cause lingering irritation.

### WEATHER

Weather in the Rockies can often be the single most important factor in determining the success (or enjoyability) of a trip. On a short-term scale, checking weather reports before leaving is as important as remembering your boots. Weather can change from bluebird skies to a full-on blizzard in a matter of hours, so always be prepared for variable conditions. Bringing a watch with a barometric altimeter is a good way to keep an eye on near-term weather; a rapid drop in air pressure is cause for getting prepared. On a longer time scale, seasons in the main ranges of the Rockies generally consist of summer from mid-July till early September (when travel on rock and wearing boots is preferred) and winter from late November till mid-May (when skis and snow slopes are in good shape). The transitions between summer and winter (often called "shoulder seasons") offer a bit of both types of travel conditions. Thankfully the front ranges are often drier than the main ranges and can offer summer-like conditions for much of the year (see the Yellowhead Highway East chapter).

### AVALANCHES

Many of the routes described in this book can be done in winter or early summer (i.e., spring) conditions, and thus avalanches are a serious concern. There is no substitute for formal avalanche training and equipment if travelling (or planning to travel) in avalanche terrain. Be sure to check Avalanche Canada at avalanche.ca for information on where to take an accredited avalanche course and how to assess avalanche danger. Other useful resources include textbooks such as *Mountaineering: The Freedom of the Hills*, published by The Mountaineers Books. If you have any doubts about the hazard of a particular slope, play it safe

Individual routes recommended in this book as winter or spring ascents are further classified by ATES ratings. These ratings describe the approximate hazard associated with particular routes and should only be treated as guidelines (e.g., even "simple" terrain can still be dangerous in extreme avalanche hazard conditions or for a "once in a hundred years" slide). Many of the routes in this book that are recommended for summer can be subject to some avalanche hazard well into the regular "summer" period in high snow years. Hazards for these routes are described to include "Early Season Avalanches." As usual with decisions in the hills, use common sense when route-finding and avoid travelling in avalanche terrain unless necessary (and then only with appropriate training and gear).

## DAY LENGTH

The Canadian Rockies experience a massive difference in length of daylight over the course of the year. For the Jasper townsite, daylight varies from almost 17 hours at the height of summer to just over 7 hours in the depths of winter. As a result, be sure to plan your routes accordingly and always take along a headlamp, especially in winter, when a few-hour delay can easily mean returning to camp in darkness.

## WATER SOURCES

What constitutes safe drinking water in the Canadian Rockies is the source of some debate. The authors have heard (and personally experienced) numerous accounts of people drinking directly from alpine streams year after year and never experiencing any ill effects. However, there are a number of illnesses, particularly giardiasis (also known as beaver fever), that can be contracted in the woods. Also present are many other types of small insect larvae and algae which can cause gastrointestinal problems in humans. Giardiasis is particularly insidious, as symptoms (persistent diarrhea, nausea, cramps) will often not appear for a week or two but may last just as long. The recommended preventive measure is to purify any drinking water before consumption (as well as water used for cleaning wounds). Acceptable methods include chemical tablets, UV light exposure or microporous filters, each method with its own benefits and limitations. Any outdoors store can point you to several options. Persons with thyroid issues should avoid using chemical tablets containing iodine. Boiling is also an acceptable method of removing biological contaminants, but it will not affect chemical or mineral deposits (which filters will remove).

## CAMPING AND BIVYS

Many trips in this book require several days to complete. When camping in the backcountry, there are a number of factors to consider in addition to what you may be used to for frontcountry (i.e., roadside) camping.

For trips in national parks, Parks Canada has the following regulations for bivouacs in backcountry areas without campsites. First, each member of a trip must obtain a backcountry camping permit, which can be purchased at a Parks Canada visitor centre. Bivy sites must be situated in alpine, unvegetated areas and must be as close to the start of the intended route as possible. Fires are not permitted at bivy sites, and any windbreaks or shelters must be taken down when leaving. As with other backcountry campsites, all garbage must be packed out, and solid human waste should be packed into a small hole dug in active soil and covered with rocks. Lastly, permits will not be granted for bivy sites within 1 km of Alpine Club of Canada huts.

Furthermore, Parks Canada has additional guidelines for backcountry winter camping ("winter" being defined as November 1 through April 30). Sites can be located anywhere so long as they are 5 km from a plowed road and 1 km from a trail. Tents must be situated so that they cannot be seen by day users of trails or defined routes. Several specific areas (Bald Hills, Spirit Island, Parkers Ridge and Whistlers Creek) are quoted as being restricted from winter camping. Fires are permitted at random campsites unless they are in the following areas: Tonquin Valley, Skyline Trail, Geraldine Lakes Trail and Jonas Cutoff. A general guideline is to talk to the visitor centre for your respective park and confirm your route descriptions before heading out.

Recommendations for Mount Robson Provincial Park and Whitehorse Wildland Provincial Park are similar to those used by Parks Canada (consult their respective information centres or websites for information on current practices).

Always remember to carry appropriate provisions and supplies for the environment you are intending to overnight in (see the **Equipment** section for suggestions). Even for day trips, bringing along a tarp or an emergency bivy sack is advised in case of unforeseen delays. When setting up a backcountry camp, aim to use the same practices you would use when frontcountry camping, such as not cooking where you will sleep or using stoves inside tents without ventilation, and being careful to store food in elevated sealed containers to avoid nibbling by snafflehounds or larger critters. And of course packing out all garbage. Often for high-elevation bivys, complexities of terrain force peakbaggers to deviate from front-country camping practices; use common sense when required.

## ILLNESS AND INJURY

Dealing with illness and injuries in the backcountry is an important topic which cannot be adequately addressed in a book such as this. The authors recommend that all backcountry travellers be familiar with first aid practices and carry appropriate supplies to deal with small injuries. As described below under **Equipment**, emergency satellite devices such as Spot and InReach are becoming increasingly prevalent in the backcountry and can form one aspect of potential rescue (but should not be relied on as a foolproof solution!). Always be aware that when in the backcountry, self-evacuation may be the only option (this is particularly relevant to folks who would consider travelling alone: are you confident that you could reverse a day-long approach on a broken ankle?). Avoid travelling into backcountry conditions if you have an illness or injury which might lead to dangerous complications. Consulting a textbook specific to wilderness medicine and first aid is highly recommended, along with formal training (see **Other sources of information** below).

## EQUIPMENT

If there is one thing for certain, peakbaggers can spend a great deal of time discussing and maintaining gear. Gear in this case contains many things: clothing, boots, poles, backpacks, skis, mountaineering axes, ropes, rock and ice protection etc. For the routes described in this book, it is assumed that any peakbagger would be carrying several layers of upper and lower body clothing (with a waterproof breathable outer layer for both areas), a backpack and appropriate footwear. In addition to this, a first aid kit, headlamp, sunscreen and water should be found in your backpack.

In terms of clothing, light porous baselayers are ideal while mid-layers of warm breathable fabric such as fleece will work well. An outer waterproof–breathable shell of Gore-Tex (or similar material) is highly recommended for any time of the year. Insulating clothing (both uppers and lowers) made of down is warm, compressible and lightweight, but be wary of getting down clothing wet as it will drastically reduce its warming capabilities.

For more involved routes (or any routes in winter), crampons and mountaineering axes may be required. These tools should only be used after training and practice. Along with these tools come the complications of ropes and harnesses. Be familiar with the workings of your particular devices before heading out.

Personal rescue devices such as satellite beacons (Spot, InReach etc.) as well as dual-band radios are options for communicating with the outside world in case of emergencies. Always remember that these are backup devices and not a substitute for the training and energy required for a self-rescue.

Deciding what type of gear to carry (and how much of it) comes with experience and is a slow skill to acquire. For routes in this book requiring less-common items (mountaineering supplies, rock gear etc.), specific recommendations have been given. These are recommendations only, and if you want to carry more or less gear (based on personal experience), that is a personal judgment.

With regard to camping and bivying along routes, pay particular attention to the weather (in terms of both temperature and conditions) and plan accordingly. In the authors' experience, a sleeping bag in the range of −7° to - 9°C has the widest range of utility in the Rockies for the spring to fall season (with the exception of low camps in the height of summer where a less insulated bag could be used). In winter, always prepare for colder conditions than forecasted; a −20°C bag is a good starting point, possibly augmented with an overbag for longer trips. Talk to experts at an outdoor gear retailer for specific recommendations. In general, down sleeping bags are preferable to synthetic in terms of warmth and weight, but they perform poorly when wet. There are a great variety of stoves available for modern camping. The authors advise using canister stoves (usually containing a blend of propane and butane) only during the summer months as many perform poorly in the winter cold (where a white-gas stove would be a better alternative).

## PERMITS

As most of the mountains described in this book reside within parks (be they national or provincial), there are several different types of permits that are required for legally climbing and camping in these areas. For Jasper National Park any person stopping in the park must purchase an entry pass. This can be obtained either at the park gates when arriving from the east, west or south or at the visitor centre in Jasper. The authors recommend purchasing a year-pass rather than numerous day-passes, unless you only plan on climbing a few peaks in a year. As of 2016, entry fees were $9.80 for an adult day-pass, $67.70 for an adult year-pass or $136.40 for a group year-pass. Furthermore, if you are planning on staying overnight in a campground (whether frontcountry or back) there are additional fees. For backcountry camping, a permit must be obtained from the visitor centre in Jasper. This can be done either in person or over the phone by calling the backcountry trail office at 780-852-6177 (be prepared for a delay of a day or two for the office to respond to your request). Random backcountry camping is subject to the restrictions described above in **Camping and bivys**. As of 2016, backcountry camping fees were $9.80 per night or $68.70 for an annual pass (valid in all of the mountain national parks).

For routes in Mount Robson Provincial Park, there are no entry fees but overnight camping along Berg Lake Trail during summer (June to September) is assessed $10 per person per night (payable at the Mount Robson visitor centre or on the BC Parks *Discover Camping* website https://secure.camis.com/DiscoverCamping/BergLakeTrail?Map). No fees are assessed for camping on the trail in winter.

As of 2016 no fees or permits are needed for entering or overnighting at the official campsites in Whitehorse Wildland Provincial Park.

## APPROACHES

Due to the remote character of the Canadian Rockies, often the approach to the mountain is half (or most) of the battle a peakbagger will undertake to reach a summit. Many of the routes described in this book require long (and often character-building) approaches through dense bushy forest and complex terrain requiring navigation (as described earlier, in the **Terrain** section). Do not underestimate the time, energy and focus required on approaches! Be sure to bring appropriate gear such as a map, compass and GPS to keep track of your progress.

## MAPS AND COORDINATES

Each of the route descriptions in this book lists a relevant set of 1:50 000 National Topographic System (NTS) maps. Copies of these maps can be obtained at outdoors stores across the region and can also be printed for personal use from Natural Resources Canada at http://geogratis.gc.ca/geogratis/en/search. Furthermore, the locations of specific features or peaks are also described by grid reference coordinates. These coordinates are derived from the Universal Transverse Mercator (UTM) system and are given using the NAD83 map datum. Coordinates are abbreviated to include only relevant information: for example, the summit of Mount Edith Cavell is described as being located at 11U 420520 5835780. This corresponds to a UTM grid reference of GR 285357. For a more in-depth description of the UTM system see some of the references given below under **Other sources of Information**. Each region covered in this book has a map showing the locations of peaks, campgrounds and other notable features. Please note that these maps are only approximate and should not be used for navigation. They are based on Canada's National Topographic System (NTS) and are copyright Her Majesty the Queen in right of Canada.

## RESPECTING THE WILD

Visitors to the Rockies often remark how wild, pristine and formidable the environment seems compared to everyday urban places. Tread lightly when passing through alpine meadows and think twice before setting up a network of cairns along an approach route. When on an approach, stick to established trails whenever possible and avoid shortcutting ("trail braiding") which further disturbs the environment. Always pack out all of your garbage (and if you come across someone else's discarded garbage in the backcountry, pack it out as well) and minimize damage to trees and shrubs while bushwhacking. It is also important to note that mountain parks are a delicate ecosystem with plants and critters clinging to life through the long Canadian winter and thriving in the short summer season. Do not disturb critters big or small; remember, you are trespassing in their home.

## OTHER SOURCES OF INFO

The savvy peakbagger knows that safe and pleasant travel in the Rockies requires a great deal of knowledge and many skills. Aspiring peakbaggers should consult many sources beyond this text to build a solid foundation of mountain knowledge. The bibliography at the back of this book is by no means exhaustive, but it should get you started in the right direction.

## DIFFICULTY RATINGS

There are numerous ways to grade the difficulty of routes in the mountain environment. In this book we chose to describe routes by three parallel grading systems. The first will be familiar to peakbaggers who have been following the seminal work of Alan Kane, *Scrambles in the Canadian Rockies*, or Andrew Nugara's *Snowshoeing in the Canadian Rockies*, which describes the difficulty of using several "common language" grades. In this book "common language" gradings are given as:

**On-trail hike:** A trip which takes you on an official trail that leads to the summit. There are no route-finding challenges to be had (unless attempting the hike in winter) and little or no bushwhacking expected. Examples of this grade include Folding Mountain and Roche Bonhomme.

**Off-trail hike:** For this grade, peakbaggers should expect straightforward terrain but little (or no) obvious trail to follow. Route-finding becomes important and patches of bushwhacking can be expected. Examples of this grade include Black Cat Mountain and The Palisades.

**Easy scramble:** An easy scramble is only slightly more involved than an off-trail hike. One can expect some rubbly terrain or other difficulties where hiking poles or hands may occasionally be used for balance. Navigational challenges and/or mild bushwhacking can be expected. Examples of this grade include Mount Cumnock and Titkana Peak.

**Moderate scramble:** For a moderate scramble, hands start to become more important for balance and often critical for short sections of low difficulty climbing. Route-finding becomes more important and often some skill is required to find the best hand and footholds. Examples of this grade include Roche de Smet and Mount Tekarra.

**Difficult scramble:** Difficult scrambles start to approach what would be described as technical climbing. Often, handholds are critical not only for balance but for weight-bearing climbing motions. Routes can often involve exposure or sustained sections (where taking a break between moves is difficult or impossible). Difficult scrambles can be exceptionally complex in poor conditions, which can escalate the route difficulty to technical mountaineering. Examples of this grade include Tripoli Mountain and Cinnamon Peak.

**Alpine climb:** In this book, any route which involves technical climbing (what would be described by the Yosemite Decimal System as 5th class; see table below) is termed an alpine climb. For these, it is usually recommended to carry a rope and appropriate climbing gear (harness, protection etc.). Alpine climbs described here are usually only a few sections of technical climbing bridged by moderate or difficult scrambles. Any alpine route description will also list a YDS grade describing the approximate difficulty. Examples of this grade include Redan Mountain and Mumm Peak.

**Mountaineering:** Several of the routes described in this volume involve travel on technical glaciated terrain. While different from alpine climbs, these routes are termed "mountaineering" with additional hazards (e.g., steep snow, crevasses, avalanche hazards) described in brackets. These are complex routes that should only be attempted by fit parties who know how to mitigate the hazards described. Examples of this grade include Mount Henry MacLeod and the north glacier route on Sunwapta Peak.

**Ski tour:** For certain parts of the Canadian Rockies, peakbagging in winter on skis allows for much more efficient travel (usually owing to frozen water bodies or a blanket of snow covering what would otherwise be an approach with intensive bushwhacking). Ski tours could be thought of as the winter equivalent of hikes, but they do have the added complications from avalanche hazards. Examples of this grade include the Miette Pass peaks.

In addition to these ratings, we have also provided two other types of grading system: the Yosemite Decimal System (YDS), terrain grades as mentioned earlier and International French Adjectival (IFA) grades. YDS describes all types of routes, from simple walks to complex big-wall climbs, by means of a number. YDS grades can be summarized this way:

| YDS GRADE | DESCRIPTION |
|---|---|
| 1 | Simple walking with few hazards. |
| 2 | Simple scrambling with occasional use of hands. Falls can lead to injuries. |
| 3 | Scrambling with necessary use of hands. Falls can be fatal. |
| 4 | Simple climbing often with exposure. Hands are essential for completion of the routes. Falls can be fatal. |
| 5 (usually including a second digit such as 5.3, 5.5, with larger numbers describing harder climbing) | Technical climbing, usually using a rope and associated equipment, often with considerable exposure or sustained sections. Unroped fall can be fatal. |

YDS grades are usually assigned only to the crux (or hardest move) on a route, so a route with a grade of 5.4 may be mostly 3rd or 4th class climbing with a single section rated at 5.4.

International French Adjectival grades describe more than just the technical difficulty of the crux of a route; they also incorporate length, overall difficulty and commitment (i.e., whether it is possible to turn around or retreat from an attempt). These ratings have become increasingly popular with guidebooks in the Rockies and BC Interior ranges and are included here for consistency. The "lower difficulty" IFA grades relevant to this book are summarized below:

| IFA GRADE | DESCRIPTION |
|---|---|
| F, *facile* (easy) | Straightforward climbing and scrambling. Can include glacier travel but limited to low-angled slopes. Retreat is also straightforward. |
| PD, *peu difficile* (slightly difficult) | Routes which involve more sustained climbing and snow and ice up to 45° can be encountered. Glacier travel can be complex. Some belaying may be required. Retreating may involve complex route-finding. |
| AD, *assez difficile* (fairly difficult) | Steep snow and ice between 45 and 60° can be expected. Belayed climbing is critical and objective hazards can be sustained. Retreating involves sustained route-finding and technical challenges. |

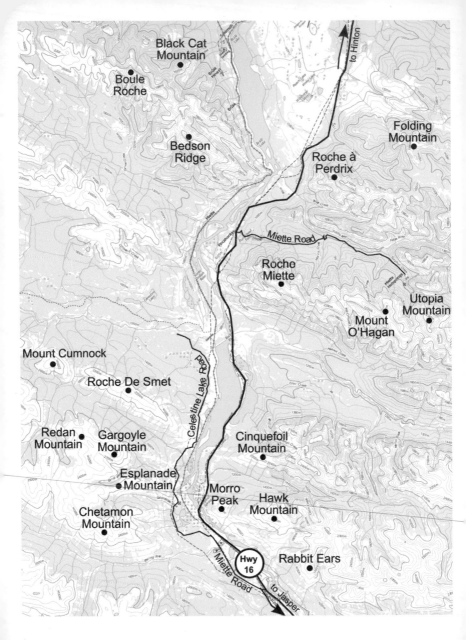

Black Cat Mountain

Boule Roche

Bedson Ridge

Roche à Perdrix

to Hinton

Folding Mountain

Miette Road

Roche Miette

Utopia Mountain

Mount O'Hagan

Mount Cumnock

Roche De Smet

Celestine Lake Road

Redan Mountain

Gargoyle Mountain

Cinquefoil Mountain

Esplanade Mountain

Morro Peak

Hawk Mountain

Chetamon Mountain

Miette Road

Hwy 16

Rabbit Ears

to Jasper

# YELLOWHEAD
# HIGHWAY EAST

| MOUNTAIN | ELEVATION (M) | ROUTE TYPE | PAGE |
|---|---|---|---|
| Bedson Ridge | 2240 | Easy scramble | 28 |
| Boule Roche | 2385 | Moderate scramble | 30 |
| Black Cat Mountain | 1801 | Off-trail hike | 34 |
| Cinquefoil Mountain | 2259 | Easy scramble | 36 |
| Folding Mountain | 2117 | On-trail hike | 38 |
| Hawk Mountain | 2553 | Moderate scramble | 40 |
| Morro Peak | 1679 | Easy scramble | 42 |
| Mount O'Hagan | 2446 | Moderate scramble | 44 |
| "Rabbit Ears" | 2070 | Alpine climb (5.2) | 46 |
| Roche à Perdrix | 2134 | Moderate scramble | 48 |
| Roche Miette | 2316 | Moderate scramble | 50 |
| Utopia Mountain | 2563 | Difficult scramble | 52 |

# SNARING AND CELESTINE LAKE ROADS

| MOUNTAIN | ELEVATION (M) | ROUTE TYPE | PAGE |
|---|---|---|---|
| Chetamon Mountain | 2606 | Difficult scramble | 56 |
| Mount Cumnock | 2460 | Easy scramble | 60 |
| Esplanade Mountain | 2301 | Difficult scramble | 62 |
| Gargoyle Mountain | 2693 | Difficult scramble | 64 |
| Redan Mountain | 2629 | Alpine climb (5.4) | 66 |
| Roche de Smet | 2539 | Moderate scramble | 68 |

## AREA OVERVIEW

The area east of Jasper boasts a large number of scenic and enjoyable summits of varying difficulty. For peakbaggers eager to emerge from winter hibernation, this part of the Rockies often gets relatively light snowfall and thus many objectives come into shape as early as May. Approaches here are generally short and many of the popular peaks have well-established trails guiding progression upwards.

While not as tall as their neighbours along the Icefields Parkway to the south, peaks here boast wide-reaching views and, on a clear day, grant excellent views of distant giants like Mount Robson.

## ACCESS, ACCOMMODATIONS AND FACILITIES

To reach this area from the east or west, take the Yellowhead Highway

(Hwy 16). It can also be approached from the south via the scenic Icefields Parkway (Hwy 93).

There are two minor roads used in this section: Celestine Lake Road and Miette Road. Check with Parks Canada in Jasper regarding the condition of these roads prior to a trip, as they can often be closed in early-season conditions.

There are two campsites that are within Jasper National Park, one along the Snaring River (Snaring), the other up Miette Road (Pocahontas). Both sites operate only seasonally and can be very busy in the summer. Reservations are recommended to guarantee a site. It also possible to stay in cabins at Pocahontas Lodge (at the start of Miette Road), in Jasper townsite at a myriad of hotels and hostels or in nearby Hinton.

Supplies can be obtained in either Jasper or Hinton (Hinton has lower prices and larger selection). There is also a restaurant at the Pocahontas cabins located at the start of Miette Road.

## PERMITS AND RESTRICTIONS

Except for Folding Mountain and Black Cat Mountain, all the trips described in this section enter Jasper National Park, and as such they are subject to restrictions. Obtain more information from Parks Canada in Jasper or from the Parks Canada website. The routes ascending Boule Roche and Bedson Ridge pass through Rock Lake Solomon Creek Wildland Provincial Park and are subject to similar restrictions as found in Jasper (though no permits are required for entering the park).

Wide-reaching views from a grassy bench north of Esplanade Mountain.

## BEDSON RIDGE, 2248 M

Difficulty:
easy scramble (2nd, F)

Hazards:
rockfall

Round-trip distance:
16 km

Total elevation gain:
1750 m

Round-trip time:
10–12 hours

Recommended seasons:
summer; fall

Map:
83F05 Entrance

*Marking the eastern edge of Jasper National Park, Bedson Ridge is home to a number of trad climbing routes on its lower slopes. The summit of the ridge itself can also be accessed via the hamlet of Brûlé.*

ACCESS: To reach Brûlé, head east past the Jasper Park gates until the junction with Hwy 40. Head north on Hwy 40, crossing the Athabasca River, then turn west onto Brûlé Road and follow it for 15 km to reach Brûlé. Park at a pullout on the north side of 2nd Street to easily access Supply Creek.

Steven Song hiking in the bed of Supply Creek. The ascent route follows the right fork of the creek, skirting left of a high patch of trees on scree and slabs.

From the middle of the ridge looking south towards the summit of Bedson Ridge (B) and the prominent unnamed peak (U).

APPROACH: From the pullout on 2nd St. head south along a gravel road/trail until you reach Supply Creek.

The route up Supply Creek will vary considerably based on water level. Usually the creek is very dry by late July/early August and should allow for quick travel up rocks and logs. Follow the creek to a junction (3 km from the parking area) and take the branch to climber's right to avoid steep terrain. Ascend higher, following the creek and eventually a mix of moss and scree to gain the ridge. Atop the ridge you should notice several park boundary signs announcing you have snuck into the park! Gaining the ridge from the boundary and traversing to the summit would require complicated scrambling on loose rock. The recommended line involves descending from the boundary ridge, heading through treed slopes, and regaining the ridge directly westwards (via the least steep line; see the routeline photo below). Once back on the ridge, keep heading upwards onto the broad summit. Descend the same way.

Difficulty:
moderate scramble
(3rd, F)

Hazards:
rockfall

Round-trip distance:
19 km

Total elevation gain:
1400 m

Round-trip time:
10–14 hours

Recommended seasons:
summer; fall

Map:
83F05 Entrance

*One of the first peaks visible when driving into Jasper National Park from the east, Boule Roche is a nice early-season outing which you are certain to have to yourself.*

ACCESS: Via Brûlé Road on the north side of the Athabasca River. To reach this road, drive 20 km east of the Jasper Park gate on Hwy 16 and turn north on Hwy 40 heading towards Grande Cache. Cross the Athabasca River and take the next left onto Brûlé Road. Carry on along Brûlé Road for 13 km and after the bridge crossing Scovil Creek, park on the north side of the road.

APPROACH: From the parking spot, start out on a faint trail following Scovil Creek. 1 km from the road the trail opens to a cutblock (GR 417088) which runs straight to GR 399106, where it intersects Oldhouse Creek. See the routeline shown in the entry for nearby Black Cat Mountain on p34.

Once on the cutblock, follow it for 2.5 km until you reach Oldhouse Creek. Bushwhack along the banks of the creek, crossing when necessary and eventually aiming to be on the south side of the stream and passing beneath the summit of Black Cat Mountain. Some 4.5 km (and 500 vertical metres) from the end of the cutblock, the bush fades to rock and proper scrambling begins. Continue upwards on scree/snow through the centre of the main gully for 400 vertical metres before angling climber's right up a steep

Looking up at the upper slopes of Boule Roche when traversing from Black Cat Mountain. The route ascends from the creek and follows the middle of the gully on scree until the summit plateau is reached.

scree slope to the summit plateau. Take note looking back at the interesting curved strata on the unnamed peak to the south. In early-season conditions, a mountaineering axe might not be out of place for lingering steep snow patches beneath the summit. The summit gives interesting views of nearby Mount Aeolus along with many unnamed peaks to the north. To the best of the authors' knowledge, a direct traverse from Boule Roche along the ridge to Mount Kephala (6 km to the north) has never been completed but looks quite spicy in places. After you finish taking in the views, descend the way you came.

POSSIBLE EXTENSION: To make it a two-peak day it is possible to ascend the west ridge of Black Cat Mountain and traverse back to the cutblock. See the route description beginning on p35 for details.

Looking east from the ascent bowl showing the direct route (D) from Oldhouse Creek or the traverse from Black Cat Mountain (B).

Difficulty:
off-trail hike (2nd, F)

Hazards:
dense bush

Round-trip distance:
10.5 km

Total elevation gain:
800 m

Round-trip time:
6–8 hours

Recommended seasons:
summer; fall

Map:
83F05 Entrance

*Black Cat Mountain got its curious name from a characteristic burn pattern near its summit that was said to resemble a black cat when seen from the nearby Canadian Pacific Railway line.*

ACCESS: Via Brûlé Road on the north side of the Athabasca River. To reach the road, drive 20 km east of the Jasper Park gate on Hwy 16 and turn north on Hwy 40 heading towards Grande Cache. Cross the Athabasca River and take the next left onto Brûlé Road. Carry on Brûlé Road for 13 km and then park on the north side of the road after the bridge crossing Scovil Creek.

Looking towards Black Cat Mountain (BC) and Boule Roche (B) from Brûlé Road on a misty morning. Both routes share an approach along a cutline before diverging up to Black Cat or staying down by Oldhouse Creek for Boule Roche.

Surprisingly nice views from the summit of Black Cat Mountain. The route up Boule Roche (B) is shown.

APPROACH: From the parking spot start out on a faint trail following Scovil Creek. At 1 km from the road, the trail opens to a cutblock (gr 417088) which runs straight to GR 399106, where it intersects Oldhouse Creek.

Follow the cutblock for 1.4 km (to around GR 407098) and then bushwhack westward, aiming for the ridge of Black Cat Mountain. Following near the crest of the ridge you should shortly come across a faint trail with occasional bits of orange flagging tape. At this point simply follow the trail upwards and enjoy the hike. Views from the summit are better than anticipated from satellite imagery and you can see nearby peaks such as Boule Roche and Kephala Mountain (as well as less lofty peaks such as the mighty Brûlé Hill to the south). Views also extend across the valley to Folding Mountain and Roche à Perdrix. It is possible to combine Black Cat Mountain with Boule Roche (described at p30), but if Black Cat is the only summit for the day, return the way you came.

POSSIBLE EXTENSION: It is possible to traverse the ridge and carry on to Boule Roche, though the bushwhacking can be quite fearsome in places. If you do carry on, descend the west ridge of Black Cat Mountain, aiming for the edge of treeline below Boule Roche and losing about 200 m of elevation. Don't lose faith while thrashing through the bush: good views and decent scrambling are only a little ways away! Once you arrive at treeline, the route joins up with the regular ascent line for Boule Roche.

Difficulty:
easy scramble (2nd, F)

Hazards:
few

Round-trip distance:
12 km

Total elevation gain:
1250 m

Round-trip time:
5-7 hours

Recommended seasons:
spring; summer; fall; winter
(snowshoes)

ATES rating:
simple

Map:
83E01 Snaring River

*Cinquefoil is an alternative name for the genus Potentilla, a group of mountain plants that look similar to strawberry bushes. While not a lofty peak, Cinquefoil Mountain offers an easy way to get into the alpine and take in some lovely views.*

ACCESS: Directly from Hwy 16. Drive 25 km east of Jasper or 25 km west from the park gate.

APPROACH: To gain the ascent ridge (which is followed for the rest of the route), take note of where the ridge drops to the highway. From the pullout a short trail (the start of the decommissioned Merlin Pass Trail) heads east towards a small lake. Stick to the climber's left (north) shore of the lake and aim for the ridge along a medley of game trails bringing you to the base of the steep slope and onwards up the ridge.

Looking across the valley from Chetamon Mountain to Cinquefoil Mountain (C). The route follows the ridge from near the highway to the summit. The further summit along the ridge is Roche Jacques (J).

ROUTE: Once on the ridge simply head upwards along alternating terrain of rock and mossy grass. It is quite common to see sheep lounging on the sunny, open slopes of the higher ridge, and once you ascend you will likely agree it is a fine place for a pleasant alpine stroll. Continuing upwards, you eventually move into scramblier terrain which, though easy, can be quite slippery in wet or snowy conditions. Reaching the summit gives great views of the impressive triangular bulk of Mount Colin along with great views across the valley towards the Celestine Lake Road peaks. Continuing along the ridge to Roche Jacques would move the difficulty into a technical rock climb. After enjoying the views (and a well deserved snack), ramble back down the way you came.

Looking up towards the summit during an early March ascent of Cinquefoil. Deep drifts made snowshoes essential.

Difficulty:
on-trail hike (2nd, F)

Hazards:
rockfall; early-season
avalanches

Round-trip distance:
16 km

Total elevation gain:
1200 m

Round-trip time:
6–8 hours

Recommended seasons:
spring; summer; fall; winter
(snowshoes)

ATES rating:
challenging

Map:
83F04 Miette

*Marking the dividing line between foothills and the front ranges, Folding Mountain is a pleasant stroll on a decent trail. Bring plenty of water on this trip.*

ACCESS: Via Highway 16. Find the trail marker, then park either on the side of the road for high clearance vehicles or at a nearby rest stop 400 m along the highway west of the trailhead.

APPROACH: The trail starts beside the highway (400 m towards Hinton from the rest stop on the north side of the highway and 600 m south of the Jasper gate's RV resort) and is marked by flagging and a wooden sign.

The very straightforward trail up Folding Mountain (F) as seen from nearby Roche à Perdrix.

Wide-reaching view from the summit of Folding Mountain, including views of Fiddle Peak (F), Roche à Perdrix (P) and Boule Roche (B).

From the highway, the trail first leads through the mixed forest before swiftly vaulting skyward and pushing up about 550 m of elevation in the first couple of kilometres. The advantage of this is you quickly get views eastwards towards Roche à Perdrix and peaks in Jasper National Park as the trail moves in and out of bush along an undulating ridgewalk. Keep following the trail until about 7.5 km from the highway, where the ridge flattens and presents a scree ramp, the only obstacle between you and the summit plateau. The scree is only an easy scramble but sturdy poles are certainly an asset for stability. In particularly snowy conditions this slope could pose an avalanche hazard. On the summit plateau, wide-reaching views await you, with the chain of peaks marking the edge of the Rockies stretching north and south to the horizon. If feeling energetic it is easily possible to keep traversing the open plateau southwards (following an old ATV trail), but most folks will enjoy the views (and a good place for lunch) and then start the plod back down, retracing their steps.

# HAWK MOUNTAIN, 2553 M ☐

Difficulty:
moderate scramble (3rd, F)

Hazards:
rockfall

Round-trip distance:
21 km

Total elevation gain:
1700 m

Round-trip time:
9–12 hours

Recommended seasons:
summer; fall

Map:
83E01 Snaring River

*As with many peaks in the Rockies, Hawk Mountain is named for a bird which happened to be flying above the summit when M.P. Bridgland ascended it in 1916.*

ACCESS: Directly from Hwy 16, 20 km east of Jasper or 30 km west of the park gate.

APPROACH: From the parking lot on the east side of the highway, go up an embankment and set off on the well-defined (Overlander) trail.

Scrambling on the ridge of Hawk Mountain on an early-season ascent.
Photo: Eric Coulthard.

The route up Hawk Mountain (H) first passes beneath Morro Peak (M) before rising upwards along a rib and straddling treeline and then entering into alpine scrambling terrain. At (C) is Mount Colin.

Follow the Overlander trail, leaving the turnout for approximately 400 m. The route gradually traverses to climber's right under Morro Peak. Carry on for 2.8 km from the trailhead before taking a sharp left up a drainage (often there is a cairn here to aid in navigation). Follow a trail which traverses gradually climber's left to break through cliff bands guarding the upper mountain. When confronted by a short, difficult rock step, take a look to climber's right to find a straightforward bypass. The trail briefly heads back into the bush before heading out onto open scrambling terrain with magnificent views. The rest of the route offers sustained scrambling of moderate difficulty with a few optional bits of more spicy manoeuvres if desired. Return the same way.

Difficulty:
easy scramble (2nd, F)

Hazards:
rockfall

Round-trip distance:
3.6 km

Total elevation gain:
650 m

Round-trip time:
3–5 hours

Recommended seasons:
spring; summer; fall

Map:
83E01 Snaring River

*Morro is Spanish for "round hill," which accurately describes this easily accessible peak. This is a short day with good views.*

Access: Directly from Hwy 16, 20 km east of Jasper or 30 km west of the park gate.

Approach: From the parking lot on the east side of the highway go up an embankment and set off on a well-defined trail.

Follow Overlander Trail (shared with the approach for Hawk Mountain) for about 400 m before gaining elevation up the west ridge of the peak. There are many well-defined trails in the area, and locating the right one can pose a navigational challenge. The correct trail starts heading up the west ridge quite quickly, and it is worth spending a few minutes ensuring you are on route before carrying on. The trail is bounded by light bush which gradually gives way to easy scrambling hopping across rocks and roots before reaching the summit marked by a distinctive large wooden cross. After you are content with trying to pick out the larger peaks on either side of the valley, return the way you came.

The trail up Morro Peak (M) as seen from Chetamon Mountain. Hawk Mountain (H) and Mount Colin (C) loom above, farther along the Colin Range. The correct trail starts heading up the west ridge quite quickly and it is worth spending a few minutes ensuring you are on route before carrying on. Recent maintenance has tried to diminish trail braiding by placing sticks and rocks to block incorrect side-trails.

Looking back down towards the highway from partway up Morro Peak. Note the well-formed maze of trails on the open slope below. The correct trail is very well defined and quickly diverges from Overlander Trail near the base of Morro Peak's west ridge.

Difficulty:
moderate scramble (3rd, F)

Hazards:
rockfall; early-season
avalanches

Round-trip distance:
10 km

Total elevation gain:
1100 m

Round-trip time:
7–10 hours

Recommended seasons:
summer; fall

Map:
83F04 Miette

*A fairly short scramble near Miette Hot Springs that affords great views of Jasper Lake and a multitude of front-range peaks near the park boundary. The views from the summit are well worth the effort and the peak can also be combined with nearby Utopia Mountain for a full day out.*

ACCESS: Via Miette Road. The trail starts at the Miette Hot Springs parking lot. Miette Road is subject to winter closure and usually reopens in April (check with Park officials to confirm before heading out).

The route up the slopes of Mount O'Hagan (O) as seen from a nearby high point.

Sulfur Skyline (S) and Utopia Mountain (U) as seen from the summit of Mount O'Hagan.

APPROACH: The trailhead lies at the south side of the parking lot Set out along a paved trail to the ruins of the original hot springs resort and carry on farther up Utopia Creek.

From the parking lot, set out on the (initially paved) trail to the original hot springs and continue following the west side of the creek. Your route will depend on the water level in the creek. Later in the year it is preferable to stay close to the creek to avoid bushwhacking through dense foliage, but this will not be possible in spring. Whichever way you decide to go, carry on some 3 km along the creek, slowly gaining elevation until you reach a prominent gully with the slopes of Utopia Mountain behind you. From the base of this gully there remains only a mere 400 m to the summit! Head up the gully on snow or scree (if in spring be wary of avalanche potential on this slope), gain the summit ridge and go on to the summit itself. If heading onwards to explore the ridge to the south, follow the directions below; otherwise return the way you came.

POSSIBLE EXTENSION: From the summit of Mount O'Hagan it is entirely possible to descend to the south and carry on to a series of unnamed peaks. If you have the energy and time, this diversion is quite pleasant and makes a nice ridgewalk to round out the day. Descend back down to the creek and return the way you came. It is also possible to connect Mount O'Hagan with Utopia Mountain, ascending the scree slope described at p53. This loop makes more sense if you start with Utopia (ascending the regular route) and climb Mount O'Hagan second.

Difficulty:
alpine climb (5.2, PD−)

Hazards:
significant rockfall; brief mild exposure

Round-trip distance:
12 km

Total elevation gain:
1100 m

Round-trip time:
4–7 hours

Recommended seasons:
summer; fall

Maps:
83D16 Jasper; 83C13 Medicine Lake

The summit block of Rabbit Ears. Crack climbing required. Numerous lines are possible, so be sure to take note of how you got up so you can get back down! Photo: Eric Coulthard.

*A mountain named unofficially for the striking resemblance of its summit towers to the ears of a rabbit. It is also known as "CR5a," as it is a subpeak of the fifth summit in the Colin Range (a surprisingly logical designation).*

ACCESS: Via Overlander Trail. Park at 6th Bridge via Maligne Lake Road.

APPROACH: Set out on Overlander Trail from the 6th Bridge parking area. Carry on for about 3 km until you reach a prominent washout and boulder field.

Head up the boulders, going left or right as appropriate. The route in this next section is approximate, based on year-to-year rockfall which can deposit massive boulders in random locations! Be swift in this section, as rockfall can be significant! Once in the gully, carry on upwards for 15–20 minutes before trending left, which will take you on a forested ridge leading to the summit. If you trend left too soon you'll reach a lower ridge which will require miserable bushwhacking to continue upwards. The final summit block involves climbing a crack system and should only be attempted in dry conditions. Take great care when downclimbing the summit block and then reverse your steps.

The way up Rabbit Ears (R) as seen from Overlander Trail on the approach. The route follows the prominent gully and then ascends the treed ridge before reaching the tricky summit block. Photo: Eric Coulthard.

**Difficulty:**
moderate scramble (3rd, F)

**Hazards:**
rockfall; early-season avalanches

**Round-trip distance:**
7.4 km

**Total elevation gain:**
1400 m

**Round-trip time:**
4–8 hours

**Season:**
spring; summer; fall

**Map:**
83F04 Miette

*This peak's official name, which translates as "Partridge Rock," refers to its foliated rock strata that resembles the game bird's tail feathers.*

ACCESS: Directly from Hwy 16 just outside the Jasper Park boundary. Park at a pullout on the south side of the highway some 800 m east of the park gate.

APPROACH: From the parking lot, set out in a clearing on a well-worn trail traversing beneath some low cliffs. After 300 m the trail moves onto the ridge and you start gaining elevation.

The first part of the route along the ridge straddles the Jasper National Park boundary as many signs are happy to inform you.

A well-formed cairn atop Roche à Perdrix, looking farther westward into Jasper National Park.

Continue on the ridge for another 1 km and 300 m of elevation (moving in and out of the park as many signs will inform you) before traversing climber's left below the north face of Roche à Perdrix. After traversing for a little less than 2 km, the route rises up a gully and follows treeline until it reaches the N/NE ridge. Once on the ridge, move steadily upwards through sparse bush until you reach a broad plateau complete with two massive summit cairns. Enjoy the views stretching far into the foothills to the east and more impressive peaks to the west. Return the way you came.

Difficulty:
moderate scramble (3rd, F)

Hazards:
rockfall

Round-trip distance:
11 km

Total elevation gain:
1400 m

Round-trip time:
4–7 hours

Recommended seasons:
summer; fall

Map:
83F04 Miette

*Roche Miette is well known to tourists driving into Jasper from the east due to its large summit plateau and steep north face (which is home to several technical climbing routes).*

ACCESS: Directly off Hwy 16. The parking lot is 37 km east of Jasper or 11.5 km west of the park gate, on the south side of the highway.

APPROACH: Follow the road from the highway for about 900 m from the parking lot; then take a sharp right and follow a trail heading up (and crossing) the creek. Be careful not to turn too early or you will be forced to sidehill and cut through bush to gain the trail. If you cross the creek while on the road you have gone too far and should backtrack about 150 m.

The route from The Notch first heads up a gully bypassing a large cliff band before aiming climber's leftward up a steep loose slope to gain the summit plateau. Photo: Eric Coulthard.

The route up Roche Miette as seen from Roche de Smet, showing The Notch (N) and the summit (M).

Once off the road and on the trail, the route follows the rising ridge for about 3 km on scree and moss up to a shallow col known as The Notch. At The Notch it is time to put on your helmet, as from here the next 350 m of elevation is on perilously loose rock. The route trends upwards to climber's left (bypassing a cliff band; see image below), soon gaining the summit plateau. Stick close together to avoid raining rocks down on your comrades.

Difficulty:
difficult scramble (4th, F)

Hazards:
rockfall; brief exposure

Round-trip distance:
15 km

Total elevation gain:
1450 m

Round-trip time:
6–9 hours

Recommended seasons:
summer; fall

Map:
83F04 Miette

*Utopia Mountain was rumoured to be so named because it was such a wonderful reprieve from the bugs of the valley below.*

ACCESS: Via Miette Road. Park at the lower lot for Miette Hot Springs; the trailhead is on the south side of the lot.

APPROACH: From the parking lot start out on a paved tourist trail which heads down along Sulphur Creek. Keep on the trail once you leave the pavement, and stay near the creek.

On the ridge near the summit of Utopia Mountain (U), the exposed (and often windy) downclimb (D) is shown.

The ascent route (A) up Utopia Mountain follows the skyline ridge to the summit (U). The alternative descent (D) down a large scree gully is fun scree skiing! The popular hike up Sulphur Skyline is also shown (S), itself a great viewpoint for looking upwards at Utopia Mountain.

After leaving the paved trail stay near the creek, and after reaching a braid in the stream, cross where convenient (which can be difficult in the spring) to the climber's left side. Look for a well-worn trail with plenty of flagging. Carry on along this until it branches left and upwards towards treeline beneath Utopia Mountain. Past treeline you will reach an alpine meadow and the start of the scrambling terrain. Scramble up the ridge on well-textured, grippy rock to gain the top of the prominent scree gully. Once past the gully, keep heading upwards on scree/snow to the summit ridge. Just before the summit a brief exposed downclimb separates you from the goal. After the downclimb the summit is only a few moderate moves away. On return it is worth considering scree-skiing down the prominent scree gully below the second ridge. Once at the bottom of the scree slope, follow the creek downwards until you regain the approach trail to continue back to the parking lot.

POSSIBLE EXTENSION: If time and energy permit, it is possible to extend the trip from the alternative descent route heading up Mount O'Hagan. If you are considering this option, read the route description on p45 and follow it from the base of the creek upwards. Follow the approach route for Mount O'Hagan to return back to the trailhead.

# SNARING AND CELESTINE LAKE ROADS

The peaks in the following pages share a common approach along Snaring and Celestine Lake roads. The following information should be consulted before setting out for these objectives.

### ROAD ACCESS

To reach Snaring Road, drive 10 km east of Jasper on Hwy 16 and turn left, following signs for Snaring Campsite. Continue on past the campsite (crossing the Snaring River) and turn left. In about 6 km you will reach the Snaring warden station; staying on the road will bring you to Corral Creek and Celestine Lake Road.

Celestine Lake Road is closed in winter and usually reopens in May (check with Jasper National Park to confirm). The road is accessed from Snaring Road, carrying on past the Snaring River after the Snaring campsite. After crossing Corral Creek (signed), the road is subject to one-way travel restrictions based on time intervals. As of 2016, travel times were listed as:

> **towards Celestine Lake:**
> 08:00–09:00, 11:00–12:00, 14:00–15:00, 17:00–18:00

> **towards Jasper:**
> 09:30–10:30, 12:30–13:30, 15:30–16:30, 18:30–19:30

The area east of Jasper can have impressive views, even from the roadside.

Travel on Celestine Lake Road is rough and often muddy, so Parks recommends high-clearance vehicles with four-wheel drive, especially if there has been any recent rainfall. Take careful note of the one-way times, as turnaround spots along the road are difficult to come by.

The routes described for Roche de Smet, Redan Mountain and Mount Cumnock share an approach up Vine Creek Trail. This track travels along the bank above Vine Creek but has not seen maintenance in many years and its two crossings of Vine Creek are without bridges. Crossing can be accomplished by rock-hopping but might be difficult during the high water of spring melt. There is a decommissioned backcountry campsite at Vine Creek, but it is not recommended, due to poor access to running water as well as being located in prime bear and mosquito habitat. In 2015 Parks conducted a controlled burn at the southern end of Roche de Smet near Vine Creek Trail.

The Snake Indian River valley marks the eastern edge of this region as seen from Beaver Bluffs. Roche de Smet (RS), Gargoyle Mountain (G), Redan Mountain (R), Whitecap Mountain (W) and Mount Cumnock (C) are shown.

## CHETAMON MOUNTAIN, 2606 M     ☐

**Difficulty:**
difficult scramble (4th, F)

**Hazards:**
rockfall; significant exposure

**Round-trip distance:**
18 km

**Total elevation gain:**
1950 m

**Round-trip time:**
14–16 hours

**Recommended seasons:**
summer; fall

**Map:**
83E01 Snaring River

*A prominent peak with a long, interesting ridge, Chetamon Mountain marks the eastern boundary of the Snaring River and gives a great view of the untamed wilds of northern Jasper as well as more familiar peaks to the south. Bring plenty of water for this peak; things can get quite dry above treeline.*

ACCESS: Via Snaring Road (see p54).

APPROACH: After passing the Snaring campsite and the Snaring River, turn left onto Snaring Road and drive just over 2 km until you reach a clearing on the left that makes a nice parking spot.

The routeline to reach the false summit (F). Starting at Snaring Road, the route bushwhacks onto the ridgecrest and follows it to the visible false summit.
Photo: Eric Coulthard.

From the clearing head westward through a clear-cut and then into the bush. Bushwhacking on Chetamon's lower slopes can be quite tight in places with ample deadfall. Continue westwards for about 1.2 km before gaining elevation on less bushy slopes leading you to the ridge. Following the ridge to treeline includes moderate scrambling that serves as a nice warm-up for the latter part of the ridge. The ridge leads upwards via mildly exposed moderate slopes trending towards the first false summit. The false summit is worth a stop if you have time but can be avoided by staying low and traversing across the west-facing slopes. Past the false summit the terrain gets trickier, with difficult scrambling along the ridge-crest and moderate to difficult (but loose) routes slightly lower. Keep following the ridge to the next high point, dropping down when necessary, until you arrive at the true summit. The last move before the summit is "airy." Don't be fooled and keep traversing farther; the next high point is an outlier of nearby Cliff Mountain and more than a scramble to reach. Descend back the way you came.

View from the false summit looking towards the true summit (S). Cliff Mountain is visible in the distant right (C). The route to Chetamon Mountain's summit follows the ridgecrest, occasionally dropping downwards to climber's left.

Difficulty:
easy scramble (3rd, F)

Hazards: rockfall and
deadfall

Round-trip distance:
30 km

Total elevation gain:
1700 m

Round-trip time:
11–13 hours

Recommended seasons:
summer; fall

Map:
83E04 Snaring River

*Rising over Vine Pass, Mount Cumnock is an often overlooked peak in the Jasper area which despite the long approach offers great views of the pristine wilderness of Jasper's north, including prime views of peaks such as Whitecap Mountain, Mount Haultain and Mount Tory. On a clear day the view of distant Mount Robson is also very impressive.*

ACCESS: Via the one-way timed-travel Celestine Lake Road (see p54).

APPROACH: Park at the Vine Creek trailhead 1.6 km east of the Corral Creek crossing on Celestine Lake Road. The route travels along Vine Creek Trail, passing the warden station and carrying on along an old horse trail towards Vine Pass.

The route up Mount Cumnock follows Vine Creek Trail all the way to the warden station (about 8 km) and then follows an old horse trail. The terrain around the pass is quite boggy and an extra pair of shoes or waterproof pants would not be out of place. The trail past the warden station can be quite hard to spot amidst the dense foliage, but once you are on it, it becomes a straightforward plod (with a fair bit of log hopping!) and soon enough you are out of the swamp and back into old forest. While passing through the trees, be mindful of where you are in relation to Mount Cumnock and do not follow the trail too far to the west. Once at a suitable location (with a good view of red rocks higher up on Cumnock), descend to the creek, cross whatever is safest and head upwards. The terrain on the Cumnock side of the creek is mostly burned-out deadfall, so a careful step is needed to avoid breaking an ankle, but otherwise there are no complications. Past the deadfall the trees give way to rocks and it is a short plod onwards to the summit. Return the way you came.

POSSIBLE EXTENSION: If you still have more energy, it is possible to descend back down to the burned-out deadfall slopes of Mount Cumnock and head up nearby "Vine Peak" as well. Descend to the Cumnock/Vine col and then head up scree slopes to the summit.

Looking towards Mount Cumnock from nearby Redan Mountain. The route travels up Vine Creek, going down into the unnamed creek between Vine Pass and Mount Cumnock before rising up through burned forest and on to the summit.

Difficulty:
difficult scramble (4th, F)

Hazards:
rockfall

Round-trip distance:
9.5 km

Total elevation gain:
1350 m

Round-trip time:
7–9 hours

Recommended seasons:
summer; fall

Map:
83E01 Snaring River

*An esplanade is defined as a long, level area, and Esplanade Mountain fits the name well, boasting a large summit well suited to enjoying fresh air and lunch after a brisk ascent.*

ACCESS: Via Snaring Road (see p54).

APPROACH: After passing the Snaring campsite and the Snaring River, turn left onto Snaring Road and drive for just over 6 km until you reach the Snaring warden station. Park far enough off to the side of the narrow road so as not to obstruct traffic.

Scrambling terrain on the upper ridge of Esplanade Mountain from an early-season (May) ascent. The summits of Esplanade (E) and Gargoyle (G) are shown.

The routeline on the upper ridge of Esplanade follows the ridgecrest upwards, occasionally dropping down to climber's left if the scrambling gets too difficult.

From the junction leading to the warden cabin, head up towards the base of the peak (careful not to disturb the wardens!). Turn left over a small creek and follow the least dense line of bush upwards towards Esplanade's ridge. Keep heading upwards for about 600 m before reaching a rocky face which can be tackled head-on or more easily bypassed to climber's left. Keep climbing along the ridge on a mix of bush and moderate rock for the next 500 vertical metres before the ridge starts to level out. At this point, bush starts to fade away and more moderate scrambling awaits. Generally, descending slightly climber's left can get around difficulties, but watch for loose rocks. The last 200 m is gained on a mix of dirt and scree which eventually yields to a broad summit with superb views of nearby Gargoyle Mountain as well as more distant peaks such as Whitecap Mountain and Mount Colin. Descend via the same route, and do not be tempted to leave the ridge early, as you would be in for quite a bushwhack!

Difficulty:
difficult scramble (4th, F)

Hazards:
rockfall; exposure;
early-season avalanches

Round-trip distance:
15 km

Total elevation gain:
2200 m

Round-trip time:
10–13 hours

Recommended seasons:
summer; fall

Map:
83E01 Snaring River

*Like its namesake statue, Gargoyle Mountain looms over the Athabasca River Valley with a watchful eye. Would-be scramblers should take heart, though: this route is much more fun than it is foreboding and is well worth the trip.*

ACCESS: Via Snaring Road (see p54).

APPROACH: Park just before Corral Creek (where Snaring Road changes into one-way Celestine Lake Road), and cross the creek on foot.

After crossing Corral Creek, follow the road for 400 m and start the ascent at a clearing on your left. A twisting network

This route up Gargoyle Mountain avoids any 5th class sections but still is full of difficult and moderate scrambling and some grovelling up very loose scree.

Looking at the upper section of Gargoyle Mountain (G) from above the first cliffband. Scree slopes are traversed to access the base of the grey rockband. The rock gets firmer from there on until the summit ridge is reached.

of goat paths leads you steadily upwards on steep dirt and loose rock to gain Gargoyle's approach ridge. There is almost 700 m of elevation gain to get atop the ridge, so be prepared for a tuff puff! Once on the ridge, keep following goat trails towards the peak for about 3 km before reaching a broad, grassy clearing. From the clearing the rest of the route comes into view. At this point you are confronted with several options, all of which involve loose rock. The most direct method is to head climber's left (descending slightly) towards a weakness and then go climber's right to a high bench (see Gargoyle upper-section photo). Keep track of your ascent route as finding the most efficient way back down can be difficult. Once you are on the bench, the rock quality improves dramatically and you are treated to 250 m of pleasantly moderate scrambling on big, solid blocks. Topping out on the summit ridge you are presented with two options to continue: either descend a chimney on climber's left and traverse towards the summit on scree, or stick to the exposed ridge. If the rock is in any way wet or snowy, taking the chimney is recommended. Either route will lead you to the summit, a decent-sized rocky bump with particularly excellent views to the north of Whitecap Mountain and, on a clear day, distant Mount Robson. Descend via the same route. If you become disoriented on descent, a broad avalanche gully facing SE can be descended from about 2280 m to treeline to regain the ridge with some elevation regain. **Do not** descend to Corral Creek, as its upper waters are plagued with dense alders.

Difficulty:
alpine climb (5.4, PD−)

Hazards:
rockfall

Round-trip distance:
22 km

Total elevation gain:
1800 m

Round-trip time:
12–14 hours

Recommended seasons:
summer; fall

Map:
83E01 Snaring River

*The most technical of the ascents around Vine Creek, Redan Mountain has both interesting climbing and far-reaching views to tempt would-be climbers.*

ACCESS: Via the one-way timed-travel Celestine Lake Road (see p54).

APPROACH: Park at the Vine Creek trailhead 1.6 km east of the Coral Creek crossing on Celestine Lake Road. The route travels along the Vine Creek trail and eventually gains the ridge.

Start up the Vine Creek trail, which generally follows the climber's right side of the creek for 8 km before reaching a swampy section near the Vine Creek warden cabin. Once in the clearing, turn climber's left and start bushwhacking up the slopes towards a prominent bump below Redan's summit. Later in the season it is possible to lessen the bushwhack by continuing north

From the summit of Redan Mountain looking towards Mount Knight (K) and Mount Thornton (T) with Mount Robson (R) visible in the distance.

From midway up the ridge the summit block can be seen. It is best tackled following the nose on steep (but good) rock until the angle mellows.

a further 300 m before turning climber's left to follow a steep drainage upwards. Once on the bump near 2300 m, lose a bit of elevation down to a col and then upwards towards a steep rockband guarding the summit. Ascending the crux rockband involves 20–30 m of a mix of difficult scrambling and a few low 5th moves for which a rope is recommended. Higher up the slope the angle eases off but the rock quality deteriorates; before you know it the summit has been reached! The summit affords great views all around with rarely glimpsed peaks such as Mounts Knight, Thornton and Rutherford in sight. Return the way you came, being careful when downclimbing the upper rock. Most parties will want to consider a 60 m rope to rappel through the steeper sections, along with slings/pitons for anchors.

Difficulty:
moderate scramble (3rd, F)

Hazards:
rockfall; brief mild exposure

Round-trip distance:
21 km

Total elevation gain:
1700 m

Round-trip time:
9–13 hours

Recommended seasons:
summer; fall

Map:
83E01 Snaring River

*At the head of the De Smet Range, Roche de Smet is a prominent long ridge northwest of Jasper Lake. While the south end of the ridge (separately named Mount Greenock) may see more traffic, the true summit grants wide reaching views of Jasper and on a clear day has an unobstructed view of distant Mount Robson as well as numerous underexplored peaks in the northern part of the park.*

ACCESS: Via one-way timed-travel Celestine Lake Road (see p54).

APPROACH: Parking is at the Vine Creek trailhead, 1.6 km east of the Corral Creek crossing on Celestine Lake Road. The route travels along Vine Creek Trail and eventually gains the ridge.

Vine Creek Trail, while often bushy and overgrown, is quite easy to follow. Views from the trail are quite limited, with occasional glimpses of Gargoyle Mountain and the ridge of Roche de Smet peeking out through gaps in the foliage. You'll want to keep an eye on where the true summit of Roche de Smet is, and not start to gain the ridge until you have passed it. The recommended route heads upwards 8.0 km from the trailhead ascending a treed face that gives way to easy scrambling to the ridgecrest. Once on the ridge, travel south towards the summit. Don't worry if the summit block looks somewhat fearsome from a distance; once you're closer, a moderate route takes shape trending up a rubbly gully yielding to the true summit itself. Once at the summit and finished with admiring the views, either descend the way you came or via an alternative gully (if dry), shown on the routeline below.

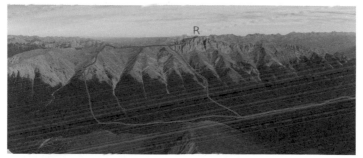

Looking towards Roche de Smet from Redan Mountain. The recommended ascent route (A), alternative descent gully (D) and summit (R) are shown.

The true summit of Roche de Smet from the ridge. Don't lose hope the summit can be accessed by a moderate scramble.

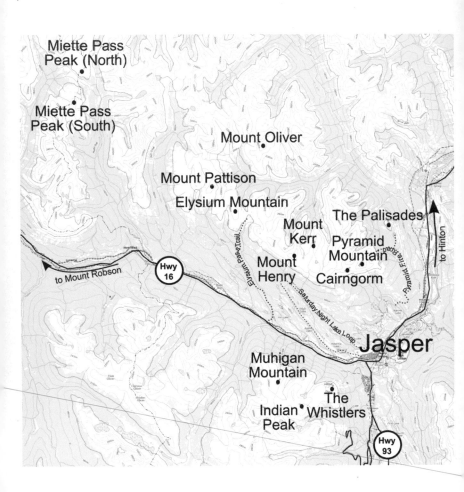

Miette Pass
Peak (North)

Miette Pass
Peak (South)

Mount Oliver

Mount Pattison

Elysium Mountain

The Palisades

Mount
Kerr

Pyramid
Mountain

to Mount Robson

Hwy
16

Mount
Henry

Cairngorm

to Hinton

Jasper

Muhigan
Mountain

Indian
Peak

The
Whistlers

Hwy
93

# YELLOWHEAD HIGHWAY WEST

| MOUNTAIN | ELEVATION (M) | ROUTE TYPE | PAGE |
|---|---|---|---|
| **The Southern Victoria Cross Range Traverse** | | Moderate scramble | 74 |
| • Pyramid Mountain | 2763 | Easy scramble | 80 |
| • Cairngorm | 2610 | Easy scramble | 82 |
| • Mount Kerr | 2630 | Moderate scramble | 83 |
| • Mount Henry | 2615 | Moderate scramble | 84 |
| The Palisade | 2100 | Off-trail hike | 86 |
| Elysium Mountain | 2446 | Easy scramble | 88 |
| Mount Oliver | 2887 | Difficult scramble | 90 |
| Mount Pattison | 2380 | Easy scramble | 92 |
| The Whistlers | 2467 | On-trail hike | 94 |
| Indian Peak | 2731 | Easy scramble | 96 |
| Muhigan Mountain | 2626 | Easy scramble | 98 |
| Miette Pass Peak (North) | 2305 | Ski tour | 99 |
| Miette Pass Peak (South) | 2272 | Ski tour | 99 |

The western side of Jasper National Park contains many less-travelled summits in areas such as the Victoria Cross Range as well as more popular routes accessed via the Jasper SkyTram. Many of the routes are amenable to winter ascents on skis or snowshoes and offer long climbing seasons. The highlight of this chapter is the Southern Victoria Cross Range Traverse, a multi-day alpine scramble which travels along the range of peaks north of Jasper townsite, starting with Pyramid Mountain and heading westwards. As with any multi-day backcountry trip, undertaking the full traverse (or part of it) should only be done by competent parties with proper planning. Be sure to call Parks (see contacts below) to sort out backcountry camping permits prior to heading out.

The terrain in the Victoria Cross Range north of Elysium Pass feels exceptionally remote.

Looking west from near the summit of Mount Kerr, the impressive bulk of Mount Bridgland rises in the middle of the frame.

## ACCESS, ACCOMMODATIONS AND FACILITIES

To reach this area from the east or west, take the Yellowhead Highway (Hwy 16). It can also be approached from the south via the scenic Icefields Parkway (Hwy 93).

The one minor road described in this section, Whistlers Road, is used to access The Whistlers trail and the Jasper SkyTram. Check with Parks for conditions of this road (as well as the highways) before setting out.

The two campsites in this area, Whistlers and Wapiti, are both accessed from Hwy 93 just south of Jasper. Both sites are subject to seasonal restrictions and can be exceptionally busy in the summer. Reservations are recommended to guarantee a spot. There are a great number of hotels in Jasper, of various levels of comfort/expense to suit any group. There is also a hostel (HI-Jasper) operated by Hostelling International located on Whistlers Road, which can be booked via hihostels.ca.

Provisions and gear of all sorts can be obtained in Jasper.

## PERMITS AND RESTRICTIONS

All of the trips in this section lie within Jasper National Park and as such are subject to restrictions. Obtain more information from Parks Canada in Jasper or at pc.gc.ca/eng/pn-np/ab/jasper/visit.aspx. Backcountry camping is restricted to specific areas; contact Parks for details.

## SOUTHERN VICTORIA CROSS RANGE TRAVERSE ☐

Difficulty:
moderate scramble (3rd, F)

Hazards:
rockfall; early-season
avalanches

Total trip distance:
~45 km
(Pyramid Fire Road to
Elysium Pass Trailhead)

Total elevation gain:
~3400 m
(Pyramid Fire Road to
Elysium Pass Trailhead)

Total trip time:
2–4 days

Recommended seasons:
summer; fall

Map:
83D16 Jasper

*An aesthetic line following the wall of peaks that rises north of the Jasper townsite. Be prepared for remote summits, peaceful valleys and many, many boulders.*

ACCESS: The southern Victoria Cross Range can be accessed via several points (of varying quality). The route described here starts at the summit of Pyramid Mountain (see p80 for route details) and is followed to the decommissioned (but still very travellable) Elysium Pass trail. Along the route it is possible to bail out (with dense bushwhacking and difficult bush navigation) to Saturday Night Lake Loop and head back to Jasper. These options are described below under Escape Routes.

Looking towards the gully below Mount Kinross.

The next part of the traverse as visible from Cairngorm, showing Mount Henry (H), Mount Kinross (K) and Snaring Mountain (S).

From the summit of Pyramid Mountain it is possible to carry on for a traverse of the Victoria Cross Range, tagging several summits along the way. This is a long traverse with considerable elevation gain and should only be attempted after thorough planning. To carry on westwards, descend the southwest ridge of Pyramid Mountain for 100 m and then cut down onto the west face, descending to the valley bottom. The route then ascends a prominent snow/scree gully below Mount Kinross to reach the next valley to the west. From this point, an ascent of Cairngorm is possible; see p82 for details.

If bypassing Cairngorm, carry on westwards across the valley, aiming for a red scree slope below Mount Kerr (see image on p83). Carry on up this slope for 300 vertical metres to reach a lovely alpine lake. If time and energy permit, it makes sense to ascend Mount Kerr and carry on with the traverse by descending the south ridge of Kerr before heading farther westwards.

From the summit of Mount Henry looking north towards the remote upper Snaring River valley.

It is also possible to bypass the summit of Cairngorm, descending into the valley (complete with more alpine lakes) and reascending steep snow/scree to reach the east ridge of Mount Henry (see the route description and image on p84), where the route continues. From the summit of Mount Henry the route descends the mountain's northwest face to the large lake to the northwest. From the lake, head up the valley to the west to gain a col at GR 127669 which allows access to the back-side of Emigrants Mountain and to Elysium Pass. The Elysium Pass trail can be gained around GR 105670, where it rises through the bush beneath Emigrants Mountain and heads back towards the highway. See the route description for Elysium Mountain on p88 for a complete description of the Elysium Pass trail.

ESCAPE ROUTES

While the town of Jasper and the Yellowhead Highway are not far in terms of straight-line distance during this traverse, it takes considerable effort to bail back to civilization. The most logical exit points are the Pyramid Mountain fire road (either ending the traverse here or backtracking, depending on your location), descending to Saturday Night Lake Loop or returning to the highway via the Elysium Pass trail. All of the described routes (unless you retrace your steps) leave you far away from your initial parking spot, so arranging pickup or stashing a bike ahead of time is critical.

Take note that the area surrounding Pyramid Lake and the Pyramid Lake fire road is subject to closure (see the approach to Pyramid Mountain at p81), so descending in the bush sw of Pyramid Mountain is not a legal (nor likely very pleasant) option.

In the valley between Cairngorm and Mount Kerr, a descent to Saturday Night Lake Loop is possible. To do so, aim for a high plateau near GR 188647 before descending 400 vertical metres on scree/snow to treeline. From there, strike out southwest, aiming for Saturday Night Lake Loop (a GPS track of the trail is exceedingly helpful here), which is some 2 km of dense, unsavoury bush away.

From the summit of Mount Henry it is also possible to descend to Saturday Night Lake Loop by sliding down loose red scree for 500 vertical metres and then fighting through dense bush for a little over 1.5 km to reach the western end of the trail. Again a GPS track (with Saturday Night Lake Loop preloaded onto your device) is exceedingly useful for properly navigating this escape route. For either of these options, it is still a long way back to Jasper (around 13 km if you reach the trail at its most westward point).

The bushwhacking about to begin to get back to Saturday Night Lake Trail.

The last of the described paths back to civilization, and the one recommended by the authors, heads from Elysium Pass along the decommissioned Elysium Pass trail with about 15 km (and 300 m of elevation regain) to get back to the highway. See p88, Elysium Mountain, for details.

**Difficulty:**
easy scramble (3rd, F)

**Hazards:**
rockfall; early-season avalanches

**Round-trip distance:**
28 km

**Total elevation gain:**
1650 m

**Round-trip time:**
9–12 hours

**Recommended seasons:**
summer; fall

**Map:**
83D16 Jasper

*Likely the most recognizable peak from the Jasper townsite, Pyramid Mountain rises 1700 m above the town and makes for an impressive sight. Much of the challenge for the mountain is mental: withstanding the 12 km one-way approach up the Pyramid fire road. Many folks will bring along a bike to make short work of the descent (but be sure to check your brakes before heading out, as they will be tested quite thoroughly!).*

ACCESS: Via Pyramid Lake Road, accessed from the Jasper townsite by turning north onto Pyramid Lake Road from Connaught Drive. Follow the road for 8 km to a gated trailhead.

APPROACH: From the trailhead, start up the wide gravel fire road. There are a couple of decent viewpoints along the approach road, but mostly you are working upward surrounded by bush. The road carries on for a little over 11 km and gains

A winter view of Pyramid Mountain from the end of the fire road. The ascent route follows the north ridge (right) to the summit.

The Pyramid fire road winds upward from Pyramid Lake Road, affording access to Pyramid itself (PY) as well as The Palisade (PA). Chetamon Mountain (C) and Esplanade Mountain (E) are also shown.

around 900 m of elevation before reaching a clearing below the east face of Pyramid Mountain. At 7.4 km, at a junction with the trail leading up to The Palisade, stick left for Pyramid Mountain. While on the approach do not leave the fire road; as of 2010 the surrounding area is subject to a legal closure as part of the Three Valley Confluence Trail Plan (see Jasper National Park's website for details).

Once the approach road has been conquered, the views start to open up and scrambling begins. Follow a well-worn trail from the road trending to climber's right up towards Pyramid's north ridge. Once you are on the ridge, the scree and dirt of the lower slopes have transitioned into moss-covered quartzite boulders that can be quite slippery if wet. While there have been reports of winter ascents of Pyramid Mountain, it is not recommended, due to this terrain. Keep following the ridgecrest to the summit. Great views of well-known peaks to the south and rarely travelled peaks to the north await you on the summit. For descent, three options present themselves: return the way you came; complete a traverse of the peak by continuing down the southeast ridge; or carry on to the west along the Southern Victoria Cross Range Traverse (described at p74). If traversing Pyramid Mountain, stick skier's right at any difficulties and eventually weave your way back down to the approach road.

## CAIRNGORM, 2610 M

Difficulty:
easy scramble (3rd, F)

Hazards:
rockfall; early-season avalanches

Round-trip distance:
3 km
(from Kinross/Unnamed col)

Total elevation gain:
300 m
(from Kinross/Unnamed col)

Round-trip time:
1.5–2 hours
(from Kinross/Unnamed col)

Recommended seasons:
summer; fall

Map:
83D16 Jasper

*The Cairngorms are a famous range of Scottish mountains which this peak is said to resemble. The summit commands a nice view across the valley and is worth the effort to ascend while following the Southern Victoria Cross Range Traverse.*

ACCESS: Via Southern Victoria Cross Range Traverse (see p74).

APPROACH: Via Southern Victoria Cross Range Traverse.

Leaving the traverse route after descending from the Kinross/Unnamed col, aim south for the low point of the ridge. Once at the base of the mountain, follow the ridge upwards, sticking near the ridgecrest for about 200 vertical metres. The summit of Cairngorm is a good place to scout out the rest of the traverse and glimpse far down the valley to the north towards the head-waters of the Snaring River. Descend the same way back to the middle of the valley and carry on with the traverse. Do not attempt to descend the southwest ridge; it is slabby and presents unnecessary difficulties.

The route up Cairngorm follows the east skyline ridge from the col to the summit. Larger boulders higher up make for moderate scrambling.

# MOUNT KERR, 2630 M

*Marking the halfway point of the Southern Victoria Cross Range Traverse (and a good place for a bivy), Mount Kerr (not to be confused with the other three Canadian peaks named Mount Kerr, all of which are in BC) boasts striking red rock that looks more Martian than Albertan. The recommended route traverses up and over Mount Kerr on the way to Mount Henry.*

ACCESS: Via the Southern Victoria Cross Range Traverse (see p74).

APPROACH: Via the Southern Victoria Cross Range Traverse.

After passing along the north shore of "Kerr Lake," continue on scree or snow until you reach the north face of the peak. Ascend via steep switchbacks (or kicking steps if there is enough lingering snow; be wary of avalanches) to the boulder-laden summit. If carrying on with the traverse from this summit, descend the south ridge of brilliant red scree and boulders before reaching the more mundane grey stone ridge leading westwards to the summit of Mount Henry.

Difficulty:
moderate scramble (3rd, F)

Hazards:
rockfall; early-season avalanches

Round-trip distance:
2 km
(from "Kerr Lake")

Total elevation gain:
250 m
(from "Kerr Lake")

Round-trip time:
2–3 hours
(from/to "Kerr Lake")

Recommended seasons:
summer; fall

Map:
83D16 Jasper

The traverse follows the northeast ridge of Mount Kerr (K) ascending from "Kerr Lake." Mount McKean (M) is visible in the distance.

Difficulty:
moderate scramble (3rd, F)

Hazards:
rockfall; early-season
avalanches

One-way distance:
4.5 km
(from "Kerr Lake")

One-way elevation gain:
600 m
(from "Kerr Lake")

One-way time:
4–6 hours
(from "Kerr Lake")

Recommended seasons:
summer; fall

Map:
83D16 Jasper

*Named for William Henry, an early employee of the North West Company in the time of David Thompson, Mount Henry offers some interesting scrambling and excellent views along a highline traverse from nearby Mount Kerr.*

ACCESS: Via the Southern Victoria Cross Range traverse (see p74).

APPROACH: Via the Southern Victoria Cross Range traverse.

The route for Mount Henry picks up from the summit of Mount Kerr (see p83). From the summit of Kerr, traverse down the south ridge on scree/boulders before reaching the gentle west ridge connecting the two peaks. Stick near the ridgecrest, briefly trending climber's right to bypass a short cliffband. The last 50 vertical metres require some moderate scrambling on loose rock. The summit is strewn with many boulders and broken rock, with one prominent feature rising a metre or so above the rest (climbing this "true summit" requires one low 5th class move). Once on the summit, rejoice, for you have finished the last of the serious elevation gain for the traverse! If weather or health is starting to turn for the worse, it is possible to bail at this point down to Saturday Night Lake Loop (see p78), but this is not recommended.

Looking up at Mount Henry from the south ridge of Mount Kerr.

Interesting rock presents scrambling opportunities near the summit of Mount Henry.

Difficulty:
off-trail hike (2nd, F)

Hazards:
rockfall

Round-trip distance:
28 km

Total elevation gain:
1250 m

Round-trip time:
7–10 hours

Recommended seasons:
summer; fall; winter
(snowshoes)

ATES rating:
simple

Map:
83D16 Jasper

*While less lofty than its neighbour Pyramid Mountain, The Palisade offers a straightforward way up into the alpine with excellent views of the eastern side of Jasper National Park. As for Pyramid Mountain, due to the length of the fire road approach during the summer, a bike approach would make for a considerably more efficient descent (but be sure to check your brakes before heading out!).*

ACCESS: Via Pyramid Lake Road, which is accessed from the Jasper townsite by turning north onto Pyramid Lake Road from Connaught Drive. Follow the road for 8 km to a gated trailhead.

APPROACH: The approach to The Palisade follows the Pyramid Mountain fire road (sharing the approach for Pyramid Mountain, p80, for the first 7.4 km).

The viewpoint before the true summit is adorned with a very large cairn, attesting to the popularity of the route.

Looking towards the true summit of The Palisade beyond the end of the official trail on a March ascent. Photo: Steven Song.

At 7.4 km from the parking area, take the right branch of the trail and continue up a less broad (but still very well-defined) trail. The trail continues for a further 4 km and 500 m of elevation gain before reaching a viewpoint with a large cairn. Here you have to decide whether bagging the true summit is on the agenda. If so, carry on along the ridgecrest through moderate bush for another 2 km and 60 m of elevation gain to a treed bump which allows for more panoramic views. Descend back the way you came.

Difficulty:
easy scramble (2nd, F)

Hazards:
early-season avalanches

Round-trip distance:
35 km
(5 km from Elysium Pass)

Total elevation gain:
1900 m
(500 m from Elysium Pass)

Round-trip time:
2–3 days (4–5 hours from
Elysium Pass)

Recommended seasons:
summer; fall; winter (skis)

ATES rating:
challenging

Map:
83D16 Jasper

*A lengthy trek up to the gates of the wilds around Elysium Pass, Elysium Mountain serves as a good introduction to the area and a fair bit of exercise on the approach. It is worth planning for several days in the area to make the approach worthwhile.*

ACCESS: The trailhead can be accessed directly from the Yellowhead Highway at the pullout shared with the Dorothy and Virl Lakes trail 13 km west of Jasper townsite (or 14 km east of the Jasper Park boundary).

APPROACH: From the trailhead carry on for about 3 km until you reach a junction. Take the branch to climber's left (climber's right leads towards Dorothy and Virl Lakes) along a more rugged (but still well-defined) trail that winds steadily upwards and westwards. The trail eventually reaches its high

Looking over towards Elysium Mountain (El), Emigrants Mountain (Em) and Elysium Pass Trail from the summit of Indian Ridge. Photo: Steven Song.

Great views of Mount Oliver (O) and Snaring Mountain (S) as well as glimpses of Whitecap Mountain (W) and Cliff Mountain (C)

Muhigan Mountain (M), Roche Noire (R), Mount Fitzwilliam (F) and Mount Bridgland (B).

point at a clearing below Emigrants Mountain 13 km from the road, then drops 200 m to Elysium Pass itself at nearly 2000 m. Allow 6–9 hours to reach the pass from the road (15 km and 1100 m of elevation gain). There is an old backcountry campsite at Elysium Pass (contact Parks for reservation details).

The route up Elysium Mountain starts at Elysium Pass and thrashes up 200 vertical metres of bush before gaining a bench. From there, trend upwards to the SE ridge and follow it up to the summit for the next 300 vertical metres. Unless carrying on westwards (described below), return the way you came, back to camp. Allow 3 hours from camp to summit.

POSSIBLE EXTENSION: From the summit of Elysium Mountain a nice full day can be spent traversing farther westwards to Mount Pattison. To do so, follow the NW ridge of Elysium Mountain for 1 km before dropping down into the valley north of a large lake. From there join up with the route described on p92 for Mount Pattison.

Difficulty:
difficult scramble (4th, F)

Hazards:
rockfall; river crossing;
early-season avalanches

Round-trip distance:
28 km
(from Elysium Pass)

Total elevation gain:
2000 m
(from Elysium Pass)

Round-trip time:
2 days
(from Elysium Pass)

Recommended seasons:
fall; winter (skis)

ATES rating:
complex

Maps:
83D16 Jasper; 83E01
Snaring River

*Named for the Hon. Frank Oliver, a politician and newsman famous for founding the Edmonton Bulletin, a prominent early newspaper in the Edmonton region in 1880. Mount Oliver is a fine peak in a remote region which can be ascended with surprisingly little bushwhacking.*

ACCESS: Via the Elysium Pass trail, described at p88.

APPROACH: Via the Elysium Pass trail. Allow 6–9 hours to reach the pass from the road (15 km and 1100 m of elevation gain).

To reach Mount Oliver without becoming hopelessly tangled in dense bush requires a rather circuitous route which stays near the edge of treeline before more open terrain can be reached. First, leave Elysium Pass heading northwards following clearings

Looking to the rest of the route up Mount Oliver (O) from an open ridge below Elysium Mountain at GR 074704. Monarch Mountain (M) is the prominent peak on the left.

The crux of the route up Mount Oliver (C) as seen from near the summit ridge, a 5.0 downclimb, can also be bypassed by losing elevation (B) and is recommended if wet or icy.

for 1.5 km. Then trend northwest for 3 km aiming to intersect a prominent open ridge at GR 074704. Once you're on the ridge, the rest of the route becomes obvious. Descend the ridge on open slopes, staying high to avoid bush, and weave your way northwards, eventually crossing Monarch Creek. Across the creek, open marshlands allow for easy access to the upper alpine. Aim to start ascending the peak by the western ridge (GR 073746). The initial section can be steep (and is an avalanche hazard if loaded), but it soon mellows to a pleasant ridgewalk. Traverse around the false summit directly ahead to reach a short connecting ridge (2400 m) that allows for passage up to the summit ridge. Sticking to the crest of the ridge is the most efficient route, but it has one complication involving a steep 5 m downclimb on slabby rock. In wet or icy conditions it would be advisable to descend beneath this cliffband and then regain the ridgecrest. Once on the summit ridge, continue upwards to the summit and take in the pristine views (especially of the sea of less-travelled peaks to the north). Return back to Elysium Pass by your ascent line.

**Difficulty:**
easy scramble (3rd, F)

**Hazards:**
rockfall; early-season avalanches

**Round-trip distance:**
15 km
(from Elysium Pass)

**Total elevation gain:**
900 m
(from Elysium Pass)

**Round-trip time:**
6–8 hours
(from Elysium Pass)

**Recommended seasons:**
summer; fall; winter (skis)

**ATES rating:**
challenging

**Map:**
83D16 Jasper

*Named for Private John George Pattison, a Victoria Cross recipient who participated in the battle of Vimy Ridge in 1917. Mount Pattison is well suited for views of Monarch Mountain and Mount Fitzwilliam.*

ACCESS: Via the Elysium Pass trail, described at p88.

APPROACH: Via the Elysium Pass trail. Allow 6–9 hours to reach the pass from the road (15 km and 1100 m of elevation gain).

The described route for Mount Pattison starts at Elysium Pass. From the pass head up into the bush southeast, aiming for a low point on Elysium Mountain's southeast ridge (GR 095658). Once over the ridge, contour northwestwards, trying to minimize elevation loss, and aim for a large lake at GR 075684. Once you are past the lake, the rest of the route presents itself (see bottom image opposite). A direct line towards the northern side of the peak is derailed by cliffs, but fear not: traversing down the slopes to skier's left and then contouring back will bring you to the base of the mountain in short order. Once on the north side of the peak, pick your way upwards on scree and boulders to the large, broad summit. On descent either return the way you came, or if you are feeling energetic, return by summiting Elysium Mountain (reverse the route described on p89).

The route up Mount Pattison (ascending the north side) from below Elysium Mountain

Wide open terrain between Elysium Mountain and Mount Pattison.

Difficulty:
on-trail hike (2nd, F)

Hazards:
early-season avalanches (via trail); few (via gondola)

Round-trip distance:
15 km (trail); 2.5 km (gondola)

Total elevation gain:
1300 m (trail); 250 m (gondola)

Round-trip time:
4–7 hours (trail); 1–2 hours (gondola)

Recommended seasons:
summer; fall

Map:
83D16 Jasper

*Likely the most visited peak in Jasper National Park, The Whistlers can be ascended over a long season either on foot or via the Jasper SkyTram and gives excellent views of the townsite and the three-valley region.*

ACCESS: Turn onto the Icefields Parkway (Hwy 93) from the Hwy 16 junction just south of Jasper townsite and after 1.8 km turn right, onto Whistlers Road. If taking the trail, turn left at 2.7 km from the Hwy 93 junction to reach the trailhead. If using the tramway, keep driving to the end of the road to the SkyTram parking lot.

APPROACH: The hiking trail is subject to avalanche hazard in the early season. Contact Parks for details before setting off. As of 2012, due to the Three Valley

Looking across the valley from Signal Mountain to the Jasper SkyTram area summits Manx Peak (M), Indian Peak (I) and The Whistlers (W). The approximate route up The Whistlers trail is also shown.

Lovely alpine terrain above the upper tram station. Photo: Vern Dewit.

Confluence Trail Plan, the area directly on either side of Whistlers Trail (Jasper Trail #5) is legally closed to all human activities. Do not deviate off the trail.

If using the trail, follow it upwards for almost 8 km to the summit. If you've taken the SkyTram, simply walk on the well-defined pathway from the upper terminal to the broad summit (you may have to fight through crowds to do so!).

POSSIBLE EXTENSION: While The Whistlers offers good views for limited effort, more adventurous folk will want to carry on to scramblier peaks in the area. Routes for Indian Peak (p96) and Muhigan Mountain (p98) are described here. If planning on extending your trip beyond The Whistlers, be mindful of the operating hours for the tramway. If you return after closing, descending the trail will be your only way back to your car.

Difficulty:
easy scramble (3rd, F)

Hazards:
rockfall; early-season
avalanches

Round-trip distance:
6 km
(from The Whistlers)

Total elevation gain:
600 m
(from The Whistlers)

Round-trip time:
2–5 hours
(from The Whistlers)

Recommended seasons:
summer; fall

Map:
83D16 Jasper

*Looming above the Jasper SkyTram, Indian Peak presents a great objective for a day in the alpine, and with the aid of the tram it can be a fairly short day. Wait for clear skies to best appreciate the view and for dry conditions to avoid treacherously slippery snow patches.*

ACCESS: Following the same routes as given for The Whistlers at p94.

APPROACH: Following the same approach as given for The Whistlers.

The route up Indian Peak starts at the summit of The Whistlers. From the summit descend the southwestern slopes along a trail, aiming for the prominent southwest ridge. Stay near the crest of the ridge, occasionally deviating around the odd boulder or loose scree patch. In early season the trail can be obscured by snow, requiring more focused route-finding. Once on the summit, take in the views and enjoy a well-deserved snack. There are several options at this point. If you wish to extend your day, a traverse of Indian Ridge is possible. For more energetic folks, carrying on westwards to the summit of Muhigan Mountain is also an option. Be sure to check your watch and gauge your time appropriately to catch the tram down or you will have to take the trail back to your car.

The route up Indian Peak (I). In dry conditions it is entirely possible to carry on with a full traverse of the ridge and return to the upper tram station. Photo: Eric Coulthard.

POSSIBLE EXTENSION: The first way to extend your day is to carry on along Indian Ridge, returning to The Whistlers. This route provides you with sustained views and simple scrambling if the ridge is dry. In early season conditions, the full traverse can be a more involved affair, and being comfortable travelling on snow (and possibly using a mountaineering axe) is essential. Add 3 km and 200 m of gain for the full traverse.

The second possible addition to this route involves carrying on west and traversing to summit Muhigan Mountain as described at p98. This will add significant time and distance to your day.

Looking down towards The Whistlers from the summit of Indian Peak on a January ascent. Winter conditions make the descent down to The Whistlers much more than a scramble.

Difficulty:
easy scramble (2nd, F)

Hazards:
rockfall; early-season
avalanches

Round-trip distance:
12 km
(from Indian Peak)

Elevation gain:
800 m
(from Indian Peak)

Round-trip time:
4–7 hours
(from Indian Peak)

Recommended seasons:
summer; fall

Map:
83D16 Jasper

*A relatively untravelled peak south of the Yellowhead Highway, Muhigan Mountain grants great views of the Victoria Cross range and the peaks of the Tonquin Valley.*

ACCESS: See the description for The Whistlers (p94) and Indian Peak (p96) for details.

APPROACH: See the description for The Whistlers and Indian Peak for details.

Ascend to the summit of Indian Peak as described. The Muhigan Mountain route starts from the summit of Indian Peak. Carry on along the ridgecrest, descending westwards from the summit for 1 km until the next high point is reached. Then descend the southwest ridge leading to the scree-filled valley below. From this point, traverse westwards, trying to minimize elevation loss, for 2 km until a gentle shoulder of Muhigan is reached. From there, sidehill for another 3 km, gradually trending upwards until the summit is reached. Take note of what time it is when you reach the summit; if planning to take the gondola back, you may have to be very hasty or else a walk down the trail will be the only way back to your car!

The route from Indian Peak to reach Muhigan Mountain (M) is quite mellow.

*Miette Pass is a prime ski touring area which has been underappreciated until recently. The route described here serves as a great introduction to the possibilities of skiing in this area in the winter.*

ACCESS: Via the Yellowhead Highway and turning onto Old Lucerne Road (30 km west of Jasper or 52 km east of the Mount Robson visitor centre). Carry on down the road until you pass the campground and reach the signed trailhead pullout just before crossing the railroad. The trailhead is equipped with a map and a register if you feel so inclined.

APPROACH: Reaching Miette Pass involves a lengthy (and complex) journey through dense bush, steep slopes and large avalanche terrain. Parties wishing to make the trek should be prepared for 20 km distance and 1600 m of elevation gain (as well

Difficulty:
moderate ski touring
(3rd, F)

Hazards:
complex avalanche terrain;
dense bush

Round-trip distance:
55 km
(both peaks)

Total elevation gain:
3100 m
(both peaks)

Round-trip time:
3–4 days

Recommended seasons:
winter (skis)

ATES rating:
complex

Maps:
83D15 Lucerne;
83E02 Resplendent Creek

Outstanding views around the Miette passes, showing Salient Mountain (S), Mount McCord (M) and the northern "Miette Pass Peak" (N).

as over 500 m of elevation loss) during the one-way trip. If planning to split the approach over two days, you will have to contact Jasper National Park for a bivy permit. Once at the pass, you have crossed the border into BC and should contact Mount Robson Provincial Park for bivy permit information. As of 2015 there are no fees currently collected for winter camping in Mount Robson Park, so if you are feeling a little cheap, make a run for the border and do the approach in a single push!

Looking back south towards Mount Fitzwilliam from the south pass.

The approach route begins by following Yellowhead Mountain Trail, which starts at the base of Yellowhead Mountain. The trail winds upwards through open forest, with the occasional clearing granting views across the valley towards Mount Fitzwilliam or up towards Yellowhead Mountain. After 6.5 km and 900 m elevation gain from the road, the trail tops out in a prominent clearing that gives you a front-seat view of a massive avalanche slope on Yellowhead's east face. From here the approach begins in earnest. There are two main navigational options: the high road (staying above treeline on large open slopes) or the low (dropping down into the bush and negotiating treed ribs). The low road is certainly safer from an avalanche perspective, as the open slopes above are directly in the line of fire from the large faces of Caledonia Mountain and Razorback Mountain above. Whichever route you choose, your general line is to head northwards, trying to maintain a constant elevation. In the trees, if you can aim for a bench near GR 948650 (at 1950 m), the bush isn't too bad and you will minimize elevation regain. Carry on until you reach the last sparsely treed rib, around GR 922674, then drop down into the valley and make your way upwards following a creek to South Miette Pass some 19 km from the highway. To cross the pass, gauge snow conditions and decide on an appropriate line. Generally the more gentle slopes on the east side of the pass are preferred to being in the crosshairs of the eastern face of Razorback Mountain. South Miette Pass marks the Alberta–BC boundary and stands at GR 884720. Once across the boundary, possible bivy sites are abundant and mostly depend on whether you are comfortable with snowmelt for drinking water. Running water is likely found lower down by the creek draining from North Miette Pass. If snowmelt sounds fine to you, camping higher gives you excellent sunrise and sunset views and is recommended by the authors. The route descriptions for North and South Miette Pass peaks given below start from the south pass.

The routes described here are for the two hills that guard the edges of North and South Miette passes. Both peaks grant outstanding views of the area and will be sure to motivate you to come back in the future for further forays into the area!

**Miette Pass Peak (South), 2272 m:** From South Miette Pass the route up the south peak is very straightforward. Aim for the eastern side of the pass, avoiding the very steep avalanche runouts descending from Razorback Mountain. Once on the ridge, trend upwards. Depending on snowcover, you may have to take your skis off and walk the final 100 m.

**Miette Pass Peak (North), 2305 m:** From South Miette Pass, descend northwards, aiming to keep as much elevation as possible and contour around the prominent ridge connecting to the south peak. Once around the ridge, you are at Centre Pass. From here, views open up and the rest of the route becomes apparent. Be certain to analyze the snowpack, as the upper slopes are quite steep and could easily slide. Aim to start up the peak using its western flank and cutting onto the steeper face when necessary. Continue heading upwards until you reach the summit. Enjoy the run back down to Centre Pass.

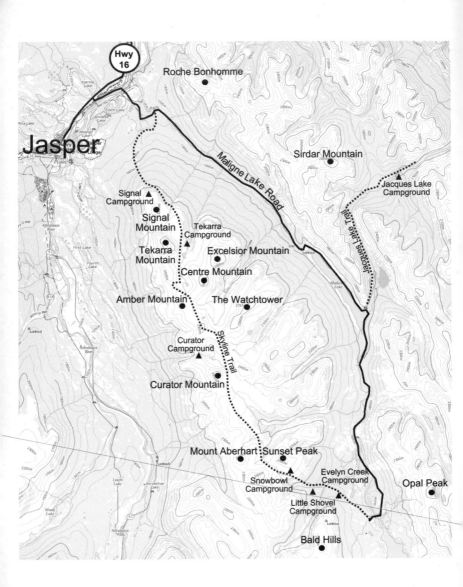

Hwy 16

Roche Bonhomme

Jasper

Sirdar Mountain

Jacques Lake
Campground

Maligne Lake Road

Jacques Lake Trail

Signal
Campground

Signal
Mountain

Tekarra
Campground

Excelsior Mountain

Tekarra
Mountain

Centre Mountain

Amber Mountain

The Watchtower

Skyline Trail

Curator
Campground

Curator Mountain

Mount Aberhart  Sunset Peak

Snowbowl
Campground

Evelyn Creek
Campground

Opal Peak

Little Shovel
Campground

Bald Hills

# MALIGNE LAKE

| MOUNTAIN | ELEVATION (M) | ROUTE TYPE | PAGE |
|----------|---------------|------------|------|
| Bald Hills | 2404 | Off-trail hike | 106 |
| Opal Peak | 2800 | Easy scramble | 108 |
| Sirdar Mountain | 2750 | Moderate scramble | 110 |
| Roche Bonhomme | 2498 | Off-trail hike | 112 |
| **Skyline Trail peaks** | | | |
| • Sunset Peak | 2415 | Easy scramble | 116 |
| • Mount Aberhart | 2510 | Easy scramble | 117 |
| • Curator Mountain | 2623 | Easy scramble | 119 |
| • Amber Mountain | 2555 | On-trail hike | 120 |
| • Centre Mountain | 2700 | Easy scramble | 122 |
| • Excelsior Mountain | 2744 | Easy scramble | 123 |
| • Mount Tekarra | 2694 | Moderate scramble | 126 |
| • Signal Mountain | 2312 | Off-trail hike | 128 |

## AREA OVERVIEW

The environs of Maligne Lake and Skyline Trail are some of the most popular areas of Jasper National Park, and for good reason! Even just driving down Maligne Lake Road and seeing the lake from the north shore is impressive. The area offers a bounty of great views with simple access, and it is a good place for a budding peakbagger to start exploring scrambling terrain.

## ACCESS, ACCOMMODATIONS AND FACILITIES
To get to this area, head east from Jasper on Hwy 16 for 1.8 km to reach

a bridge spanning the Athabasca River. Cross the bridge and head left along Maligne Lake Road. Maligne Lake itself lies 46 km down the road, while Medicine Lake (the trailhead for Sirdar Mountain) and the northern end of Skyline Trail are at 25 km and 8.9 km respectively. In winter the road may be closed for extended periods due to avalanche hazard, so be sure to check road conditions before setting out.

As the start of Maligne Lake Road is only a short drive from downtown Jasper, staying at a hotel or bed and breakfast in town is quite feasible. For those planning on more luxurious accommodations, Jasper Park Lodge shares the same bridge over the Athabasca River as Maligne Lake Road. A more frugal option is to stay in the HI Maligne Canyon Hostel (11.5 km from Jasper along Maligne Lake Road). There is also a range of campsites in the area, including Jacques Lake, six campsites directly along the Skyline trail (see p114) and three boat-accessed campsites on the lake itself. There is no camping currently permitted on the north shore of the lake. In winter, the Maligne Lake Ski Club operates the Shangrila cabin (see malignelakeskiclub.ca for details on approach and fees).

Provisions and gear of all sorts can be obtained in Jasper. Snacks can also be found at Maligne Lake Chalet (see brewster.ca/attractions-sightseeing/maligne-lake-cruise/dining-shopping for information) or the gift shop located across from the Maligne Canyon hostel.

## PERMITS AND RESTRICTIONS

All of the trips in this section are located in Jasper National Park and thus

There are many options for simple or challenging routes around Maligne Lake in summer and winter.

Maligne Lake is one of the most popular places in the Canadian Rockies and a sublime setting for alpine views.

are subject to restrictions. Obtain more information from Parks Canada in Jasper or from the Parks Canada website. Backcountry camping is restricted to specific areas; contact Parks for details.

Since 2014 the Maligne Lake area has been subject to legal closure from the start of November until the end of February to decrease predator access to caribou habitat.

## BALD HILLS, 2404 M □

**Difficulty:**
off-trail hike (2nd, F)

**Hazards:**
early-season avalanches; prime bear terrain

**Round-trip distance:**
13 km

**Total elevation gain:**
700 m

**Round-trip time:**
3–5 hours

**Recommended seasons:**
summer; fall

**Map:**
83C12 Athabasca Falls

*Likely the best views for your effort in the Maligne Lake area. With a wide, well-maintained trail leading into the alpine there will be plenty of views (and tourist traffic) on the Bald Hills throughout the summer. In winter on skis the area can feel much more remote and tranquil, though prone to avalanche hazard.*

ACCESS: Via Maligne Lake Road. Drive to the south end of the road at Maligne Lake and park in the lot. The signed trailhead is on the west side of the road.

From the trailhead, carry on up the wide road (paying attention to the other signed intersections comprising the network of trails accessible from this point). Around 2.5 km from the trailhead there is a signed

The actual high point of Bald Hills (slightly farther than the officially signed high point).

The trail is quite easy to follow and travels through open areas great for views (and bears!).

junction branching steeply upwards to climber's left. Taking this branch will save you 1 km on the trail but it is steep and slippery if wet. The trail winds steadily upwards through several switchbacks before opening up into the alpine and granting great views of Maligne Lake and the surrounding peaks. While the official trail ends at about 5 km it is very worthwhile to continue following the trail southward to the actual high point. After enjoying a snack and snapping many pictures, head back down the trail.

**Difficulty:**
easy scramble (2nd, F)

**Hazards:**
rockfall; early-season avalanches

**Round-trip distance:**
10.8 km

**Total elevation gain:**
1050 m

**Round-trip time:**
6–9 hours

**Recommended seasons:**
summer; fall

**Maps:**
83C12 Athabasca Falls;
83C13 Medicine Lake

*A very scenic peak with a good approach trail. Opal Peak is also home to some of the most enjoyable scree-skiing rock around (keep that in mind as you slog towards the summit). This is prime bear terrain, however, so be sure to check with Parks before setting off, to see if any bear warnings or trail restrictions are in effect.*

ACCESS: Via Maligne Lake Road. Drive to the south end of the road at Maligne Lake. The best parking lot for this peak is on the northeast.

APPROACH: From parking, set out on Opal Hills Trail. When you come to the Opal Hills/Mary Schäffer Loop junction, stay left and continue gaining elevation.

The loop up Opal Peak (O) as seen from Sunset Peak, with Leah Peak (L) and Samson Peak (S) also shown.

Looking towards Maligne Lake from the northern branch of the Opal Hills trail, with Mount Charlton (C) and Mount Unwin (U) dominating the view. Photo: Mike Mitchell.

At 1.5 km you will come to another junction. Take the trail to the right, which leads up to the Opal/Unnamed col rising above and enters the alpine about 2.5 km (and 440 m of elevation gain) from the trailhead. The peak is best traversed, and it is recommended to ascend from the south and descend to the north.

Once you are in the alpine, route options are plentiful. Pick your way up the west face of Opal Peak, aiming for the visible col. If the face is still snowy, be wary of avalanche hazard. From the col there is still 300 m of elevation to the summit, on easy scree via a well-worn path. Don't forget to look back towards the lake while you ascend, as the views are exceptionally lovely. Be wary of cornices along the summit ridge which can persist well into the summer. From the summit, descend easy scree on the north ridge of the peak to reach another Opal/Unnamed col. At this col, descend 150 m to gain the northern branch of the Opal Hills loop, which can be followed back to the trailhead.

**Difficulty:**
moderate scramble (3rd, F)

**Hazards:**
rockfall; early-season
avalanches

**Round-trip distance:**
29 km

**Total elevation gain:**
1700 m

**Round-trip time:**
11–15 hours

**Recommended seasons:**
summer; fall; winter
(snowshoes)

**ATES rating:**
complex

**Map:**
83C13 Medicine Lake

*While it is likely the most difficult to access of all the peaks described in this chapter, Sirdar is the highest summit in the Colin Range and a worthy objective in the Jacques Lake area. The prospect of a fair bit of bushwhacking should ensure you have the peak to yourself.*

ACCESS: Via Maligne Lake Road. Drive 25 km from Jasper to reach Medicine Lake. The pullout for Sirdar Mountain is the Jacques Lake (and South Boundary Trail) parking lot on the north side of Medicine Lake, just after a prominent bend in the road.

APPROACH: From the trailhead follow the Jacques Lake trail for 9 km, diverging shortly after the trail hooks to the northeast. Branch off to climber's left up into the bush, gaining the valley that descends from Sirdar Mountain.

The bushwhacking can get rather dense in places just below treeline.
Photo: Steven Song.

The route up Sirdar Mountain along the Jacques Lake trail before following the unnamed creek (dotted line) towards the base of the peak.

After leaving the trail, head upwards to a forested rib at around 1660 m elevation. Follow this rib westwards up the valley, paralleling the creek. Depending on conditions, fording the creek to the climber's right (north) bank may yield less dense bush. Carry on up the valley until about 12 km from the trailhead, where a broad, north-facing, treed slope grants access to the alpine bowl above. There are patches of krummholz in this area which are especially troublesome if wet or snowy. Once you are above treeline, there is still 700 m of elevation to go! Ascend the west face of the peak, initially on rock and moss which then yields to more scrambly rock above. Aim to gain the summit ridge slightly to climber's left of the true summit, but be wary of a cornice in snowy conditions. Nothing on the face is trickier than moderate scrambling, but some perseverance is required. Return the way you came.

Difficulty:
off-trail hike (2nd, F)

**Hazards:**
rockfall; early-season avalanches

Round-trip distance:
10 km

Total elevation gain:
1300 m

Round-trip time:
5–7 hours

Recommended seasons:
summer; fall

Map:
83C13 Medicine Lake

*Due to its characteristic shape, Roche Bonhomme (also known as Old Man Mountain) is one of the most identifiable peaks around the Jasper townsite and a straightforward way to a good viewpoint.*

ACCESS: Via Maligne Lake Road. Drive to the large Maligne Canyon parking lot 11.5 km east of Jasper.

APPROACH: From the parking lot, walk back on Maligne Lake Road for 350 m until you reach a large cairn on the north side of the road marking the start of a good trail.

The route up Roche Bonhomme (R) as seen from Signal Mountain. Hawk Mountain (H), Mount Colin (C) and Grisette Mountain (G) are also in view.

Looking down towards the town of Jasper from the summit of Roche Bonhomme.

Once on the trail, head upwards initially along forested flats before starting to steeply gain elevation beside a creek. The dirt on the trail can be especially slick when wet, so giving the route a while to dry off before attempting it may be a good idea. Higher up, the route breaks into the alpine, fading to easy scree slopes as the views start to improve. Once in the alpine, carry on upwards along several worn scree paths before reaching the ridgecrest. From the ridge a half-kilometre walk leads to the summit.

**Difficulty:**
easy scramble (3rd, F)

**Hazards:**
rockfall; early-season avalanches

**One-way distance:**
44 km

**Total elevation gain (south to north):**
1410 m

**One-way trip time:**
2+ days

**Recommended seasons:**
summer; fall; winter (skis)

**ATES rating:**
complex

**Maps:**
83C12 Athabasca Falls;
83C13 Medicine Lake

*Widely described as the best multi-day hike in the Jasper region, the Skyline is the best-known and best-maintained backcountry trail in the park. For the peakbagger the trail offers comfortable access to numerous summits in the area, with a good balance between remoteness and convenient access.*

ACCESS: Via Maligne Lake Road. There are two trailheads for Skyline Trail. The southern trailhead (the normal starting point) is at Maligne Lake, 46 km southeast of the Jasper townsite. The northern trailhead is 8.9 km southeast of Jasper, also along Maligne Lake Road.

APPROACH: From either parking area the trail can be easily reached via signed trailheads. Take note of restrictions and warnings on the trailhead signs, as portions of the route can be closed during certain periods.

See *The Canadian Rockies Trail Guide*, by Brian Patton and Bart Robinson, or information from Parks Canada for a full description of the Skyline. This chapter focuses on ascending peaks in the area and assumes that scramblers are starting at one of the official campgrounds along the trail. Many of the peaks in this section (particularly those near either trailhead) can also be done as long day trips.

Hiking the Skyline trail. Photo: Vern Dewit.

CAMPSITES: There are six campgrounds on the Skyline trail that can be used by hikers and scramblers. All of the sites are extremely busy in the summer and you should contact Parks for reservations before setting out. Campsites can be reserved many months in advance. Note that fires are banned at all of the sites and no dogs are allowed on the trail. The campgrounds from south to north (with distances from the Maligne Lake trailhead) are:

**Evelyn Creek**, 5 km, 4 tents
**Little Shovel**, 8 km, 8 tents
**Snowbowl**, 12 km, 8 tents
**Curator**, 19 km, 8 tents
**Tekarra**, 30 km, 8 tents
**Signal**, 35 km, 4 tents

**Difficulty:**
easy scramble (2nd, F)

**Hazards:**
rockfall; early-season avalanches

**Round-trip distance:**
3.2 km (from Little Shovel Campground)

**Total elevation gain:**
350 m (from Little Shovel Campground)

**Round-trip time:**
1.5–2 hours
(from Little Shovel Campground)

**Recommended seasons:**
summer; fall; winter (skis)

**ATES rating:**
simple

**Map:**
83C12 Athabasca Falls

*A short side trip off the Skyline trail, Sunset Peak is best done as either an evening trip after reaching Little Shovel Campground or as a detour while heading along the Skyline. The peak can also be ascended in winter as a decent ski tour.*

ACCESS: Via Maligne Lake Road and Skyline Trail (see p114).

From Little Shovel Campground carry on 1.6 km along the Skyline trail before branching off to climber's right along brush and scree slopes on the south face of Sunset Peak. Continue upwards for 200 vertical metres to gain the summit ridge pretty much at the true summit. Descend the way you came to regain the Skyline.

A winter ascent of sunset peak. The route meanders up the gentle face in the centre left of the image.

Sunset Peak is a nice viewpoint for looking back towards Maligne Lake.

*A longer but more scenic trip than Sunset Peak, Mount Aberhart is another worthwhile summit along the Skyline trail that can be ascended with few complications. The peak is especially enjoyable in winter, on skis or snowshoes, with good lines leading back to the Skyline and much sparser crowds.*

ACCESS: Via Maligne Lake Road and Skyline Trail (see p114).

APPROACH: If heading for Mount Aberhart from the south it makes the most sense to camp at Little Shovel Campground and climb the peak from there. If carrying on along the Skyline trail, camping at Snowbowl is more reasonable.

From Little Shovel Campground carry on along the trail for 2.5 km until you reach the broad pass between Trowel Peak and Sunset Peak. From here leave the trail, contouring to climber's left while trying to avoid unnecessary elevation losses. Gain the north ridge of Mount Aberhart by ascending a broad rock slope to gain the ridge at around 2320 m. Once on the ridge, head upwards for the remaining 200 m of elevation gain. Difficulty will depend on snow coverage, but in dry conditions this is an easy scramble. From the summit there are excellent views across the valley towards Mount Edith Cavell as well as the other peaks in the Maligne Range and the hordes traversing the Skyline trail below. Return the way you came.

**Difficulty:**
easy scramble (3rd, F)

**Hazards:**
rockfall; early-season avalanches

**Round-trip distance:**
11 km (from Little Shovel Campground)

**Total elevation gain:**
500 m (from Little Shovel Campground)

**Round-trip time:**
3–4 hours (from Little Shovel Campground)

**Recommended seasons:**
summer; fall; winter (skis)

**ATES rating:**
challenging

**Maps:**
83C12 Athabasca Falls, 83C13 Medicine Lake

MALIGNE LAKE MOUNT ABERHART

From Snowbowl Campground it is possible to gain the north ridge at a lower point (closer to the campground), but this route can be hazardous in deep snow, as it is steeper and more avalanche prone. If conditions are dry, scramble up to gain the ridge (moderate scramble) and intersect the Little Shovel route at the 2320 m plateau.

Looking up at Mount Aberhart (A) from the Skyline trail in winter. The described route heads up the rocky rib at centre before gaining the skyline ridge. The alternative route from Snowbowl Campground meets up on the ridge plateau (P).

Mount Aberhart is a good viewpoint for peaks like Mount Edith Cavell (E) on the other side of Hwy 93.

*A worthwhile detour from the Skyline trail at Big Shovel Pass, this peak was so named because it was thought to be the keeper (or curator) of the area.*

ACCESS: Via Maligne Lake Road and the Skyline trail (see p114).

APPROACH: While the nearest place to stay overnight is the aptly named Curator Campground, most scramblers will approach Curator Mountain from the south along the Skyline trail. Setting off from Little Shovel Campground, proceed north until you reach Big Shovel Pass 4 km away.

Once at Big Shovel Pass, trend westwards on scree towards the peak. Your route will depend on the amount of snow on the peak. If conditions are dry, you can switchback up the ridge, while if snowier, deviating to climber's left or right may be required. Once joined up with the wider southeast summit ridge, simply head upwards to reach a large cairn. Descend the way you came to regain the Skyline.

**Difficulty:**
easy scramble (2nd, F)

**Hazards:**
rockfall; early-season avalanches

**Round-trip distance:**
3 km
(from Big Shovel Pass)

**Total elevation gain:**
300 m
(from Big Shovel Pass)

**Round-trip time:**
3–5 hours
(from Big Shovel Pass)

**Recommended seasons:**
summer; fall

**Maps:**
83C12 Athabasca Falls;
83C13 Medicine Lake

Approaching Big Shovel Pass (P) with Curator Mountain (C) looming above. The route follows the skyline ridge from the pass. Photo. Vern Dewit.

Difficulty:
on-trail hike (2nd, F)

Hazards:
rockfall; early-season
avalanches

Round-trip distance:
10 km
(from Curator Campground)

Total elevation gain:
500 m
(from Curator Campground)

Round-trip time:
3–5 hours
(from Curator Campground)

Recommended seasons:
summer; fall; winter (skis)

ATES rating:
simple

Maps:
83C12 Athabasca Falls;
83C13 Medicine Lake

*This is one of the most logically named peaks in the Maligne Lake area, as its summit plateau is covered in amber-coloured shale. The summit itself can be accessed by only a short diversion from the trail.*

ACCESS: Via Maligne Lake Road and the Skyline trail (see p114). The peak is about halfway between Curator and Tekarra campgrounds (5 km and 400 m of elevation gain from Curator; 6 km and 450 m from Tekarra).

APPROACH: From either campground, follow the Skyline trail until you are directly beneath the peak.

From the Skyline, head up a well-worn path in the scree to the summit. A more adventurous line (and less crowded) can connect Amber Mountain to nearby Centre Mountain by descending the northeast ridge towards a false summit between Amber and Centre.

Looking towards the summit of Amber Mountain with Skyline Trail clearly visible. Photo: Vern Dewit.

Looking up at Amber Mountain in early-season winter conditions from a tarn below nearby Centre Mountain. Photo: Steven Song.

**Difficulty:**
easy scramble (2nd, F)

**Hazards:**
rockfall; early-season
avalanches

**Round-trip distance:**
8.5 km
(north/south traverse from
Tekarra Campground)

**Total elevation gain:**
700 m
(north/south traverse from
Tekarra Campground)

**Round-trip time:**
4–6 hours
(north/south traverse from
Tekarra Campground)

**Recommended seasons:**
summer; fall

**Maps:**
83C12 Athabasca Falls;
83C13 Medicine Lake

*The middle peak along the ridge connecting Amber Mountain to Excelsior Mountain. Centre Mountain is a worthwhile detour from the Skyline trail that can be ascended with few complications.*

ACCESS: Via Maligne Lake Road and the Skyline trail (see p114).

APPROACH: Follow the Skyline to Tekarra Campground, which is the best starting point for an ascent of Centre Mountain.

Centre Mountain can be climbed by way of several different routes. Access from the north along the connecting ridge to Excelsior Mountain entails an easy scramble transitioning from easy walking to boulder hopping as you gain the 200 m from the Excelsior/Centre col (see image on p124). For this route, go 600 m along the trail before heading east on open slopes leading towards the col. Approaching from the south along the ridge connecting Amber Mountain yields similar terrain with much boulder hopping. Stay on the trail for 3 km until you arrive beside a picturesque alpine tarn. Leave the trail and head northeast to gain the south face of the peak. If doing a traverse of the mountain, it is recommended to ascend from the north and descend to the tarn to regain the trail. Centre Mountain can be combined as the midway point of a traverse between Amber Mountain and Excelsior Mountain.

*The highest peak in the Maligne Range, named from the Latin word* excelsus, *meaning "lofty."*

ACCESS: Via Maligne Lake Road and the Skyline trail (see p114).

APPROACH: Via the Skyline trail. Tekarra Campground serves as the best base-camp for Excelsior Mountain (see p122 for access details).

From Tekarra Campground, trend east until you hit treeline and then aim for the broad, rocky west face of the peak. Once on the face, carry on upwards, hopping between boulders, to gain the summit. The peak can be nicely combined into a loop by descending the south ridge to regain the lower slopes and the Skyline trail. Excelsior can also be easily combined with nearby Centre Mountain into a larger loop by following the connecting ridge south to the Excelsior/Centre col and carrying on to the summit of Centre Mountain (see the route on p122) for more details.

**Difficulty:**
easy scramble (2nd, F)

**Hazards:**
rockfall; early-season avalanches

**Round-trip distance:**
6.5 km
(from Tekarra Campground)

**Total elevation gain:**
700 m
(from Tekarra Campground)

**Round-trip time:**
4–5 hours
(from Tekarra Campground)

**Recommended seasons:**
summer; fall

**Maps:**
83C12 Athabasca Falls;
83C13 Medicine Lake

MALIGNE LAKE EXCELSIOR MOUNTAIN

Centre Mountain as seen from Excelsior Mountain. The route ascends near the crest of the ridge towards the summit. Photo: Steven Song.

The northern peaks of the Skyline trail: Excelsior Mountain (E), Centre Mountain (C), Amber Mountain (A) and Mount Tekarra (T). Photo: Eric Coulthard.

The terrain on Excelsior Mountain is full of boulders. The ascent route follows the broad west face. Photo: Steven Song.

**Difficulty:**
moderate scramble (3rd, F)

**Hazards:**
rockfall; early-season avalanches

**Round-trip distance:**
8 km
(from Tekarra Campground)

**Total elevation gain:**
600 m
(from Tekarra Campground)

**Round-trip time:**
4–6 hours
(from Tekarra Campground)

**Recommended seasons:**
summer; fall

**Maps:**
83C12 Athabasca Falls;
83C13 Medicine Lake

*Possibly the most aesthetic peak in the Maligne Range, Mount Tekarra is often admired from the Icefields Parkway, where it rises 1600 m from the valley floor. The peak itself is a good trip from nearby Tekarra Campground, especially when done as the finale of a traverse of the Skyline trail.*

ACCESS: Via Maligne Lake Road and Skyline Trail (see p114)

APPROACH: From Tekarra Campground, head back south along the Skyline trail for 1 km before branching off to climber's right, aiming for the broad, east-facing scree and boulder face connecting Mount Tekarra and Amber Mountain.

At the base of Mount Tekarra (T), after traversing the ridge, the route trends left to avoid the cliff bands. Photo: Steven Song.

Looking towards Mount Tekarra from near the summit of Amber Mountain
Photo: Vern Dewit.

Once at the base of the rock face, scramble upwards amidst the ever-present Maligne Range boulders, aiming for the low point of the south ridge that leads to the summit of Mount Tekarra. Carrying on towards the summit after reaching this ridge requires bypassing cliffbands by heading to climber's left (and losing elevation). Descend while keeping an eye on the large scree face above leading towards the summit. Scramble through a short rockband, trending left to avoid the cliffbands above. Reach the scree and then carry on upwards. As you head upwards, two summits will present themselves: the lower summit, to climber's left, has a weather station, while the slightly higher one, to climber's right, is the true, cairned, summit. Return the way you came.

**Difficulty:**
off-trail hike (2nd, F)

**Hazards:**
rockfall

**Round-trip distance:**
5 km
(from Signal Campground)

**Total elevation gain:**
300 m
(from Signal Campground)

**Round-trip time:**
2–3 hours
(from Signal Campground)

**Recommended seasons:**
summer; fall

**Maps:**
83C12 Athabasca Falls;
83C13 Medicine Lake

*One of the more visible peaks from the Jasper townsite, Signal Mountain is so named because its broad open upper plateau was used as a base for signal fires by a nearby Hudson's Bay Company fort.*

ACCESS: Via Maligne Lake Road and the Skyline trail (see p114 for details).

APPROACH: The route starts at Signal Campground accessed via the Skyline trail.

Head 100 m south of the campground to a junction of the Skyline trail with an old fire road. Stay on the road and head upwards to the broad, open plateau that comprises the summit of Signal Mountain. After 500 m leave the road and head upwards (climber's left) to gain slightly higher terrain. Carry on a further 1.5 km to reach the high point.

The true summit of Signal Mountain in view with Mount Tekarra in the background.

Most of the route up Signal Mountain (S) from Maligne Lake Road is on a good, wide fire road. Nearby are Excelsior Mountain (EX), Centre Mountain (C) and Mount Tekarra (T).

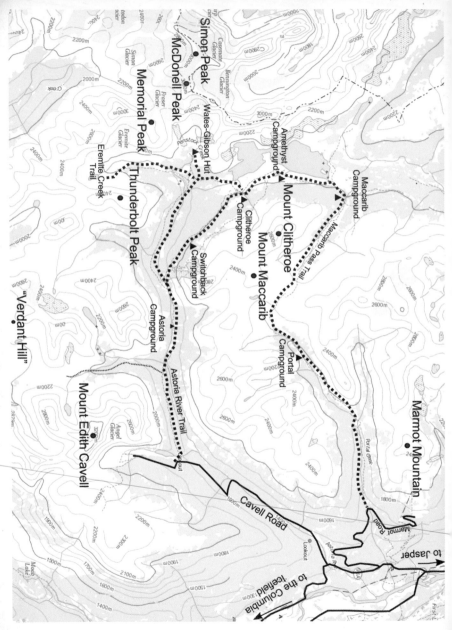

Simon Peak

McDonell Peak

Memorial Peak

Thunderbolt Peak

Simon Glacier

C Creek

Fraser Glacier

Cosmate Glacier

Bennington Glacier

Eremite Glacier

Eremite Creek Trail

penstock creek

Wates-Gibson Hut

Amethyst Campground

Clitheroe Campground

Mount Clitheroe

Maccarib Campground

Maccarib Pass Trail

Switchback Campground

Mount Maccarib

Astoria Campground

"Verdant Hill"

Astoria River Trail

Portal Campground

Portal Creek

Mount Edith Cavell

Angel Glacier

Marmot Mountain

Marmot Road

to Jasper

Cavell Road

Lookout

to the Columbia Icefield 300m

Moab Lake

First L

# TONQUIN VALLEY

| MOUNTAIN | ELEVATION (M) | ROUTE TYPE | PAGE |
|---|---|---|---|
| Mount Clitheroe | 2748 | Moderate scramble | 138 |
| Mount Edith Cavell | 3363 | Moderate scramble | 140 |
| Mount Maccarib | 2655 | Moderate scramble | 142 |
| Memorial Peak | 2870 | Alpine climb (5.3) | 144 |
| Thunderbolt Peak | 2670 | Moderate scramble | 146 |
| Simon Peak | 3322 | Mountaineering | 148 |
| McDonell Peak | 3275 | Mountaineering | 150 |
| "Verdant Hill" (GR 263652) | 2205 | Off-trail hike | 152 |

## AREA OVERVIEW

The Tonquin Valley is one of the true jewels of Jasper National Park, an approximately 500 km² area complete with alpine lakes, vast meadows and of course The Ramparts towering 1000 m above the cool waters of Amethyst Lake. A trip into the Tonquin Valley should be on the agenda for any peakbagger exploring the Jasper region. Due to the abundance of standing water in the area, fall or winter ascents can often be preferable to avoid the scourge of mosquitos that normally inhabit the region.

## ACCESS, ACCOMMODATIONS AND FACILITIES

The Tonquin Valley is usually entered by way of either the Astoria River trail or the Maccarib Pass trails. To reach either trailhead, drive 6.7 km south of Jasper along Hwy 93 to Marmot Road.

For the Astoria River trailhead, follow Marmot Road for 5.1 km from the highway and turn left (southwest) onto Cavell Road. Drive 12.5 km along Cavell Road to the HI Mount Edith Cavell hostel and park in the roadside lot on the right directly across from the hostel. Note that Cavell Road is usually closed and trackset during ski season, however, so you'll have to take that extra 12.5 km of distance and 500 m of elevation gain into account for winter ascents via this route. Take heart, though: the hostel remains open in winter, allowing for a good stopping point on the first day of an Astoria-based route (see hihostels.ca/edithcavell for booking details).

The Maccarib Pass trail starts at the Portal Creek trailhead, which is accessed by following Marmot Road for 8.8 km until a prominent bend. The trailhead is on your left, on the south side of Portal Creek (the north side is a staging area for horse activity in the region). Marmot Road is open year-round, and once the creek has frozen over, it is the preferred way to access the northern side of the Tonquin in winter.

There are seven campgrounds, a backcountry hut, a backcountry lodge, cabins and a hostel in the area, so plenty of options exist for accommodations of all degrees of luxuriousness. One of the most comfortable (and interesting) places to stay in the area is Wates–Gibson Hut. Operated by the Alpine Club of Canada, the hut is a welcome shelter in both summer and winter and is described here as the base of several routes. The hut is most efficiently accessed via the Astoria River trail, which is then followed onto the ACC Wates–Gibson Hut trail (see below for distances). For booking information, contact the ACC at (403) 678-3200 or alpineclubofcanada.ca. Check with the visitor centre in Jasper for current booking information and policies for the backcountry campgrounds in the area.

For most peakbaggers the trail system in the Tonquin Valley is most useful as it connects the official campgrounds and Wates–Gibson Hut to both trailheads. The most important parts of the network are the Maccarib Pass trail, the Astoria River trail, the Wates–Gibson Hut trail and the Surprise Point trail. Relevant distance markers for these trails are given below. For specific information about a particular trail, refer to a topographic map such as Gem Trek's "Jasper & Maligne Lake" or NTS 83D9 Amethyst Lakes and 83D16 Jasper.

## Maccarib Pass Trail

| | |
|---|---|
| 0 km | Portal Creek Trailhead |
| 8.5 km | Portal Creek Campground |
| 12.2 km | Maccarib Pass |
| 19.3 km | Maccarib Campground |
| 22.6 km | Amethyst Campground |
| 23.8 km | Tonquin- Amethyst Lake Lodge |
| 25.9 km | Clitheroe Campground and junction with Astoria River and Surprise Point trails |

## Astoria River Trail

| | |
|---|---|
| 0 km | Astoria River Trailhead (HI Edith Cavell hostel) |
| 4.0 km | junction with Verdant Pass Trail |
| 6.7 km | Astoria Campground |
| 8.2 km | junction with Wates- Gibson Hut Trail |
| 13.2 km | Switchback Campground |
| 16.6 km | Clitheroe Campground and junction with Maccarib Pass and Surprise Point trails |

## Wates–Gibson Hut Trail

| | |
|---|---|
| 0 km | Wates -Gibson Hut (UTM 11U 415091 5835485) |
| 1.2 km | junction with Eremite Valley Trail |
| 1.6 km | junction with Surprise Point Trail |
| 7.9 km | junction with Astoria River Trail |

## Surprise Point Trail

| | |
|---|---|
| 0 km | Chrome Lake and junction with Wates–Gibson Hut Trail |
| 2.0 km | Surprise Point Campground |
| 4.3 km | Clitheroe Campground and junction with Maccarib Pass and Astoria River trails |

Food, supplies and gear can be obtained in Jasper.

## PERMITS AND RESTRICTIONS

All of the trips in this section lie within Jasper National Park and thus are subject to restrictions. Obtain more information from Parks Canada in Jasper or from their website. Backcountry camping is restricted to specific areas; contact Parks for details. Fires are not allowed at any campsites in the Tonquin Valley.

The Tonquin Valley is home to a herd of caribou. As of 2014, Parks Canada implemented a "delayed winter access" policy for the region to reduce the number of human-caused threats to the animals. As a result, the Tonquin Valley is legally closed for a portion of the winter season. Confirm with Parks as to the status of this closure before planning any winter activities in the region.

Amethyst Lakes and The Ramparts are certainly one of the highlights of this region.

Looking east towards Mount Edith Cavell (in distance at centre) from Maccarib Pass Trail.

## MOUNT CLITHEROE, 2748 M ☐

**Difficulty:**
moderate scramble
(3rd, F)

**Hazards:**
rockfall; early-season
avalanches

**Round-trip distance:**
4.5 km
(from Clitheroe
Campground)

**Total elevation gain:**
700 m
(from Clitheroe
Campground)

**Round-trip time:**
3–5 hours
(from Clitheroe
Campground)

**Recommended seasons:**
summer; fall

**Maps:**
83D09 Amethyst Lakes;
83D16 Jasper

*Quite possibly the best viewpoint around for looking across to The Ramparts and down on Amethyst Lake. An ascent of Mount Clitheroe is quite the trek as a day trip but a more reasonable adventure from one of the campgrounds around Amethyst Lake.*

ACCESS: Via Astoria River Trail (see p132).

APPROACH: The most direct route to Mount Clitheroe begins at the logically named Clitheroe Campground (17 km and 600 m of total elevation gain from the Astoria River trailhead).

From Clitheroe Campground the south face of the peak offers a straightforward route to the summit. Set a course to the northeast, crossing rock-laden flats and

Characteristic terrain near the ridgecrest of Mount Clitheroe. Be careful of loose rocks near the edge.

TONQUIN VALLEY MOUNT CLITHEROE

Leading up the broken south face of Mount Clitheroe, the route follows the prominent gully shown.

aiming for a prominent gully in roughly the middle of the summit ridge (see picture above). Conditions in the gully range from loose scree to pleasant snow (a June ascent would normally still have enough snow for glissading). In dry conditions be sure to stick close together, as rockfall can be a significant concern. At the first large junction of the gully, about 400 m from the base of the peak, stay to climber's left. At a second junction, 50 m higher, take the right-hand branch. While not obvious from below, the true summit lies slightly to climber's right of the top outlet of the gully. You'll need only a few moderate moves to reach the top. Returning back down the gully is the preferred descent line.

# MOUNT EDITH CAVELL (WEST FACE/RIDGE), 3363 M □

**Difficulty:**
moderate scramble (3rd, F)

**Hazards:**
rockfall; early-season avalanches; ice patches; cornices

**Round-trip distance:**
29 km

**Total elevation gain:**
1950 m

**Round-trip time:**
14–18 hours

**Recommended seasons:**
summer; fall

**Map:**
83D09 Amethyst Lakes

*While usually a descent route for the traverse of Mount Edith Cavell, the west face and upper ridge can also serve as a less technical way to a great summit and will certainly be on the agenda for peakbaggers in the area. This is a very long day trip, so be sure to budget your time accordingly (setting out on the trail in the dark will likely be required).*

ACCESS: Via the Astoria River trail (see p132).

APPROACH: Follow the Astoria River trail for 4 km until you reach an unsigned junction with the old Verdant Pass Trail.

The west face of Mount Edith Cavell is quite loose, and numerous cliffbands make for difficult navigation.

Looking down from the northwest ridge of Mount Edith Cavell to the ascent valley below.

Once on the Verdant Pass trail, follow it for just under 4 km through forest which yields to vast open meadows. The trail winds around the west flank of Mount Edith Cavell, eventually leading to a prominent viewpoint well positioned to scope out the west face. Be sure to take a look across the valley towards Throne Mountain and the curious shape of Chevron Mountain. From the viewpoint follow a faint scree trail, first aiming for a prominent break in the cliffbands and then ascending upwards. An ascent line generally trending toward climber's right is advisable, though lingering snow patches or runoff may alter what's best. Use your head and keep track of your course while working upwards (as regaining the proper route can be considerably more difficult on descent). Once on the ridgecrest, follow it higher while aiming slightly climber's right to avoid difficulties near the summit. The route briefly crosses onto the south face directly below the summit (look for cairns), after which the ridge is followed to the cairned true summit. Be sure to follow your tracks back down to avoid being blocked by the many cliffbands on the west face.

Difficulty:
moderate scramble (3rd, F)

Hazards:
rockfall; early-season
avalanches

Round-trip distance:
29 km

Total elevation gain:
1500 m

Round-trip time:
11–14 hours

Recommended seasons:
summer; fall; winter (skis)

ATES rating:
complex

Maps:
83D09 Amethyst Lakes;
83D16 Jasper

*Although they are only a brief diversion from the official trail through Maccarib Pass, the excellent views of The Ramparts and Oldhorn Mountain make an ascent of Mount Maccarib very worthwhile.*

ACCESS: Via the Portal Creek trailhead (see p132).

APPROACH: From parking, the trail starts on the south side of Portal Creek (the trail on the north side is for horse staging and quickly meets up with the main track). The route quickly crosses over to the north side of the creek on a good bridge and leads upwards towards the Tonquin Valley. In winter or high snow conditions, you can sometimes start directly in Portal Creek, but otherwise stay on the trail until the creek is well bridged and then carry on upstream.

Follow the Maccarib Pass trail as it winds upwards until you reach Maccarib Pass (12 km and around four hours from the trailhead). Once at the pass, head up the north face of Maccarib (trending climber's right to minimize difficulties) until you join the south ridge. Be careful just below the ridgecrest, as many of the large boulders and rocks are very loose. Once you are on the ridge, follow the crest to a prominent false summit that offers great views of nearby Oldhorn Mountain. From the false summit, stay on the ridgecrest and head southeast to reach the true summit, dropping lower on climber's left when needed. Once on the summit (after of course enjoying the views!), you can either return the way you came or work your way down boulders and scree on the east face to reach Amethyst Lake and rejoin the trail network. From the base of the scree slope, the Clitheroe campground is a mere 2 km away. Mount Maccarib could be combined with the described route for nearby Mount Clitheroe from the bowl beneath Maccarib (see p138 for details).

The route up Mount Maccarib (M) from Maccarib Pass as seen from the summit of Mount Clitheroe. The alternative descent towards Amethyst Lake is shown in green. The impressive Mount Edith Cavell (EC) and Oldhorn Mountain (O) can also be seen.

**Difficulty:**
Alpine Climb (5.3, PD−)

**Hazards:**
rockfall; early-season avalanches

**Round-trip distance:**
9 km
(from Wates–Gibson Hut)

**Total elevation gain:**
950 m
(from Wates–Gibson Hut)

**Round-trip time:**
6–8 hours
(from Wates–Gibson Hut)

**Recommended seasons:**
summer; fall

**Map:**
83D09 Amethyst Lakes

*A less-travelled summit quite near Wates–Gibson Hut, Memorial Peak is a good introduction to the Fraser Glacier area and is only a half-day from the hut. Given the texture of its rock, Memorial is best climbed in dry conditions, and some parties may appreciate a rope and some slings to rappel the technical sections.*

ACCESS: Via the Astoria River trail (see p132).

APPROACH: Via Wates–Gibson Hut (see p132).

After leaving the hut, follow Surprise Point Trail north until you reach the flats below Surprise Point. Stick on the southeast side of the lake until you reach the start of the large boulder and scree slope leading

Looking over to Memorial Peak (M) from Fraser Glacier. Throne Mountain (T), Mount Edith Cavell (EC) and Blackhorn Mountain (B) are also shown.

On the northwest ridge of Memorial Peak looking up to the summit. The route follows the ridgecrest. Photo: Eric Coulthard.

up towards Fraser Glacier. Ascend for about 400 vertical metres, being careful to stay away from the toe of the glacier as you work your way around the northwest ridge of Memorial Peak. Once on the south side of the ridge, strike upwards on the ridgecrest. The crest is mostly a mix of moderate and difficult scrambling, but there are two sections of low 5th class climbing: one at a prominent false summit, the other just before the true summit. The second crux can often consist of a steep, exposed snow slope and should be approached with caution. Staying on the ridge is the best way to descend the peak. Some parties may rappel one or both of the crux sections.

Difficulty:
moderate scramble (3rd, F)

Hazards:
rockfall; early-season
avalanches

Round-trip distance:
18 km
(from Wates–Gibson Hut)

Total elevation gain:
875 m
(from Wates–Gibson Hut)

Round-trip time:
10–12 hours
(from Wates–Gibson Hut)

Recommended seasons:
summer; fall; winter (skis)

ATES rating:
complex

Map:
83D09 Amethyst Lakes

*So named because the broken summit seems to have been hit by lightning, Thunderbolt Peak is a fine day trip from Wates–Gibson Hut as a scramble or ski tour. The route described here via the Eremite Valley is somewhat circuitous but does manage to minimize bushwhacking.*

ACCESS: Via the Astoria River Trail (see p132).

APPROACH: Via Wates–Gibson Hut (see p132).

From the hut, head east towards Chrome Lake for 1.2 km until you reach a junction with Eremite Creek Trail, just before Chrome Lake. Take this trail and follow it southwards, higher up the valley, first passing marshy flats before eventually emerging into the alpine around Arrowhead Lake (a mere 4 km from the junction). Past

A duo ascending the final slopes to the summit of Thunderbolt Peak on a chilly spring day.

The route up Thunderbolt Peak (T) from Wates-Gibson Hut (WG) as seen from the summit of Mount Clitheroe. A bushy alternative winter descent is shown in green.

the end of the trail, carry on upwards to the southwest. Stay just above treeline and contour back to the southwest directly below Thunderbolt Peak's ridgeline across mossy flats and a smattering of alpine ponds. Carry on northwards, following a rocky bench until you come to the base of a scree/boulder slope at the northern end of the bench (2250 m). Steeply ascend scree for 300 m until the terrain briefly flattens before a final steep scree/snow slope granting access to the "shattered" summit. On descent the most pleasant path is to retrace your steps and return along Eremite Creek Trail. Alternatively, with good snowcover throughout the lower-level bush, a more direct line down (see the route picture above) is to head northwards from the base of the scree slope, aiming for Chrome Lake. Closely spaced trees on steep slopes make for a technical (though quick) descent if on skis!

Difficulty:
mountaineering (glacier travel; steep snow; 4th, PD)

Hazards:
avalanches; crevasses

Round-trip distance:
14 km
(from Wates–Gibson Hut)

Total elevation gain:
1400 m
(from Wates–Gibson Hut)

Round-trip time:
10–13 hours
(from Wates–Gibson Hut)

Recommended seasons:
winter (skis)

ATES rating:
complex

Map:
83D09 Amethyst Lakes

*The highest peak in the Mount Fraser massif, and not far from 11,000er status, Simon Peak boasts astounding views and is a great ski/ climb day trip from nearby Wates–Gibson Hut for those comfortable on steep snow slopes. This is the most technical route described in this section and requires knowledge of avalanche hazard, glacier travel and mountaineering axe self-arrest.*

ACCESS: Via the Astoria River trail (see p132).

APPROACH: Via Wates–Gibson Hut (see p132).

From the hut, descend to Outpost Lake and traverse to the base of the broad slope leading southwards up to Fraser Glacier. The slope climbs for some 400 vertical metres before the terrain starts to ease off and views of the surrounding peaks open up. Continue upwards, keeping to climber's right to avoid possible icefall from Outpost Peak, and gain a bench at 2500 m that marks the start of the glacier. There are numerous holes on Fraser Glacier, so parties should rope up. Aim to gain the ridge of McDonell Peak to climber's right of an unnamed subpeak (see image below of the route to Simon Peak from Wates–Gibson Hut; the ascent line goes behind Bennington Peak). Unless snow conditions are especially ideal, it is likely a good idea to leave your skis at the base of the ridge and bootpack upwards, eventually staying

Accessing the summit ridge and false summit (F) of Simon Peak via this route requires a steep snow traverse and should only be attempted in good snow conditions.

on the western side (climber's left). About 100 vertical metres below the summit of McDonell Peak, the route diverges for Simon Peak out onto the broad west face. This is a very big slope with large consequences for a fall. Take great caution in analyzing snow conditions before committing to the face, and if in any doubt, redirect to McDonell Peak instead. If snow conditions are good, traverse the face aiming for the broad summit ridge leading to the visible (false) summit as shown in the image above. Once on the ridge, be careful to stay off the large cornice as you work your way upwards. Aim to bypass the false summit to its (climber's) left and carry on upwards to the true summit. Return via the same route. Keep an eye on your watch and be careful when planning your ascent, as the west face of McDonell gets considerable sun on warm spring days and could make for treacherous snow conditions on return.

As seen from Oldhorn Col, the route to Simon Peak (S) from Wates–Gibson Hut (WG) meanders upwards, gaining Fraser Glacier before passing behind Bennington Peak (B).

**Difficulty:**
mountaineering (glacier travel; 4th, PD−)

**Hazards:**
avalanches; crevasses

**Round-trip distance:**
12.4 km
(from Wates–Gibson Hut)

**Total elevation gain:**
1400 m
(from Wates–Gibson Hut)

**Round-trip time:**
7–9 hours
(from Wates–Gibson Hut)

**Recommended seasons:**
summer; fall; winter (skis)

**ATES rating:**
complex

**Map:**
83D09 Amethyst Lakes

*This is the most accessible peak on the Mount Fraser massif. An ascent of McDonell is a worthwhile day trip involving glacier travel, scrambling and likely exposed snow slopes. A spring ascent, including a good run back to the hut, is particularly enjoyable!*

ACCESS: Via Astoria River Trail (see p132).

APPROACH: Via Wates–Gibson Hut (see p132).

Follow the route from the hut to the upper Fraser Glacier as described for Simon Peak on p148. Once above the glacier, follow the south ridge upwards, staying near the crest and then dropping below to the west side of the ridge. With about 100 m of elevation to go, several rockbands will stand between you and the summit. The difficulty of the peak will depend on the amount and type of snow coverage. It is advisable to stay along the top of the ridge. The last 50 m of elevation can involve considerable exposure on scree or snow.

Enjoying some turns while returning to the hut after a spring ascent of McDonell Peak.

Looking up towards McDonell Peak from below Outpost Peak. Considerable crevasses lurk beneath the snow on Fraser Glacier below the summit ridge.

The last 200 vertical metres of McDonell Peak (M) hold most of the technical difficulty, particularly when snowy. The diverging routeline to Simon Peak is shown in green.

**Difficulty:**
off-trail hike (2nd, F)

**Hazards:**
creek crossings

**Round-trip distance:**
27 km

**Total elevation gain:**
1000 m

**Round-trip time:**
10–13 hours

**Recommended seasons:**
summer; fall; winter (skis)

**ATES rating:**
challenging

**Map:**
83D09 Amethyst Lakes

*While by no means a lofty summit, this hill above Verdant Pass is an excellent viewpoint for Mount Edith Cavell and distant peaks on the nearby Hooker Icefield.*

Access: Via the Astoria River Trail (see p132).

Approach: Follow the Astoria River trail for 4 km until you reach an unsigned junction with the old Verdant Pass trail.

At the junction, take the Verdant Pass trail and continue until it ends in open meadows. The track winds around the west flank of Mount Edith Cavell, eventually leading to a prominent viewpoint well positioned to view all of Mount Edith Cavell, Throne Mountain and the curious shape of Chevron Mountain.

Looking up towards "Verdant Hill" from below the west face of Mount Edith Cavell.

The Verdant Pass junction is quite visible from the main Astoria River Trail.

After the viewpoint, the route diverges from the west ridge of Mount Edith Cavell and carries on towards Verdant Pass. Head south, reaching the bottom of the northwest ridge that descends from Edith Cavell, crossing a small creek and then intersecting a cairned trail. Continue heading south to reach a lake between Edith Cavell and Verdant Peak. Lose elevation down to the meadows below, aiming to intersect the creek that descends from the lake. Then cross the creek and continue south. After passing a small lake, lose about 100 m to the bottom of Verdant Pass. Aim to gain the hill on the west side. From the base of the pass it is 150 m to the summit. Return the way you came.

Chevron Mountain (left) and Throne Mountain (right) are both impressive peaks near Verdant Pass.

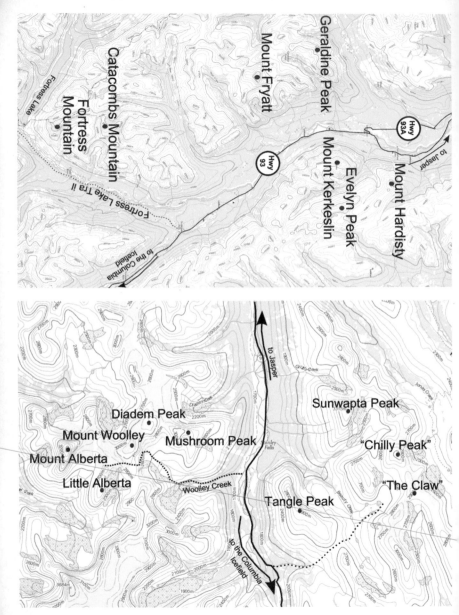

Fortress Lake

Fortress Mountain

Catacombs Mountain

Mount Fryatt

Geraldine Peak

Fortress Lake Trail

to the Columbia Icefield

Hwy 93

Mount Kerkeslin

Evelyn Peak

Hwy 93A

to Jasper

Mount Hardisty

to Jasper

Grizzly Creek

Sunwapta Peak

Diadem Peak

Mount Woolley

Mushroom Peak

Stanley Falls

"Chilly Peak"

Mount Alberta

Little Alberta

Woolley Creek

"The Claw"

Tangle Peak

Beauty Creek

Jonas Creek

to the Columbia Icefield

# ICEFIELDS PARKWAY

| MOUNTAIN | ELEVATION (M) | ROUTE TYPE | PAGE |
|---|---|---|---|
| Catacombs Mountain | 3290 | Mountaineering | 158 |
| Fortress Mountain | 3008 | Difficult scramble | 162 |
| Evelyn Peak | 2851 | Easy scramble | 164 |
| Mount Hardisty | 2761 | Easy scramble | 166 |
| Geraldine Peak | 2930 | Moderate scramble | 168 |
| Mount Fryatt | 3361 | Alpine climb (5.4) | 170 |
| Sunwapta Peak (N Glacier) | 3315 | Mountaineering | 172 |
| Sunwapta Peak (SW Face) | 3315 | Easy scramble | 174 |
| Tangle Ridge | 3000 | Off-trail hike | 176 |
| "Chilly Peak" (GR 845986) | 3090 | Easy scramble | 178 |
| "The Claw" (GR 856957) | 2980 | Moderate scramble | 180 |
| Mount Woolley | 3405 | Mountaineering | 182 |
| Diadem Peak | 3375 | Mountaineering | 186 |
| Mushroom Peak | 3210 | Moderate scramble | 190 |
| Little Alberta | 2963 | Mountaineering | 192 |

## AREA OVERVIEW

There are few other roadways in the world that are as beloved by tourists, mountaineers and peakbaggers alike than the Icefields Parkway, Hwy 93. The Parkway is a 230 km road stretching from Jasper to Lake Louise which travels through some of the most impressive terrain in the Rockies. For peakbaggers, the Parkway is primarily used as an access route enabling one to drive right to the base of many impressive peaks and to the trailheads of many more. In this chapter we restrict ourselves to peaks between Jasper in the north and the Columbia Icefield in the south. Routes described here range from straightforward scree bashes to full-on glacier mountaineering. The more complex routes, to be undertaken safely, require careful logistical planning as well as training in technical mountaineering. Thankfully, the easier objectives do still have marvellous views and allow one to appreciate the surroundings.

## ACCESS, ACCOMMODATIONS AND FACILITIES

There are three entrances to the Icefields Parkway: the northern end, accessed just south of Jasper from the Yellowhead Highway; the southern end, starting just north of Lake Louise on Hwy 1; and from the east from Rocky Mountain House through Nordegg via Hwy 11 at Saskatchewan Crossing, roughly 150 km southeast of Jasper (or 80 km north of Lake Louise). There is also one minor road described in this section: Hwy 93A, part of the original road between Jasper and Lake Louise. The south section of Hwy 93A is relevant to peakbaggers and is accessed from the north at the turnoff for the Marmot Basin ski hill, some 7 km south of the junction of Hwy 93 and Hwy 16, and from the south at Athabasca Falls.

Options for accommodations on the Icefields Parkway abound, with campsites (for conventional tents as well as RVs), roadside lodges and hostels all available for booking. As peakbaggers are often frugal folk, the Parks campgrounds or the HI wilderness hostels are the better bets. See the visitor centre in Jasper or the websites for the park (pc.gc.ca/eng/pn-np/ab/jasper/index.aspx) and the HI hostel (hihostels.ca/westerncanada/1539/Wilderness-Hostels/index.hostel) for details on availability and ways to reserve spaces.

Snacks and food can be obtained at the Icefields Centre and Saskatchewan Crossing from April to October. Unless money is no object, it is very advisable to bring all your food and supplies from elsewhere or stock up in Jasper before setting out.

## PERMITS AND RESTRICTIONS
All of the trips in this section are located in Jasper National Park and thus are subject to restrictions. Obtain more information from Parks Canada in Jasper or from their website. Backcountry camping is restricted to specific areas; contact Parks for details.

A serene sunset at a tarn below Catacombs Mountain.

## CATACOMBS MOUNTAIN, 3290 M ☐

Difficulty:
mountaineering (glacier
travel; steep snow; 3rd, F)

Hazards:
rockfall; dangerous river
crossings; crevasses;
early-season avalanches

Round-trip distance:
51 km

Total elevation gain:
1700 m

Round-trip time:
2–3 days

Recommended seasons:
summer; fall

Maps:
83C12 Athabasca Falls;
83C05 Fortress Lake

*An unlikely name for a mountain, since catacombs were underground cemeteries particularly common during the Roman Empire. Fear not: good views rather than ghostly caverns await you on this peak.*

ACCESS: Via Hwy 93. Park at the Sunwapta Falls trailhead (directly behind the Sunwapta Falls resort) on the west side of the Icefields Parkway 55 km south of Jasper or 98 km north of Saskatchewan Crossing. Follow the signs for Fortress Lake Trail, which leads southwards from the parking area across a bridge over Sunwapta Falls.

APPROACH: Via Fortress Lake Trail. The trail is wide, easy to follow and often maintained but is lacking in viewpoints. The authors recommend doing the 15 km approach to the Athabasca Crossing campground on the first evening of a trip, for more comfortable temperatures while hiking the trail. There used to be a small suspension bridge that allowed for a simple crossing of the Athabasca River, but in October 2014 the bridge was destroyed and there are currently no plans to replace it. As a result, access to Hamber Provincial Park and Catacombs Mountain has been complicated. The authors recommend bringing along a packraft for the crossing, as the river is usually too fast and deep to allow for a safe ford. Once across the Athabasca, follow the old Fortress Lake trail (expect significant deadfall and debris due to the lack of trail maintenance) for 2 km until the Chaba River can be seen on your right (west of the trail). The aim is to reach the alpine valley between Fortress Mountain and Catacombs Mountain. Crossing the Chaba can be an involved process weaving back and worth along sandbars to avoid very deep sections; do not underestimate the danger of this crossing, and only attempt it in low flow conditions. After crossing the Chaba, bushwhack upwards, staying to climber's left of the large gully descending from the valley above. The bush lets up after 3 km and 750 metres of elevation and you emerge into an alpine wonderland with astounding views of the Winston Churchill Range to the east, the north face of Fortress Mountain to the south and two lovely alpine lakes right ahead. Carry on to the upper of the two lakes, around GR 503079. The alpine area nearby makes a sublime place for a bivy.

From the upper lake, ascend the mossy scree ledge system immediately to the north to reach the edge of the glacier. Aim for the gully (often running with a decent-sized stream) on climber's left which allows for access on moderate scrambling terrain to a large bench just before the glacier. There are serious holes on Catacombs Glacier (which seems nearly large enough to be considered a small icefield), so roping up is essential. Once on the glacier, ascend in a rising traverse towards climber's right until you reach the shoulder of a gentle ridge. From here, the rest of the route becomes more evident (see images next page); contour around the first false summit before reaching the final snow slope to the summit. Be sure to stay roped while snapping summit pictures, as there are numerous crevasses on the summit itself! Return to the bivy lake the way you came. For reversing the approach, be sure to get an early start to reach the river crossings while they are lower, for increased safety.

The route to the summit of Catacombs Mountain (C) follows the grassy slopes up to the gully just climber's right of the shadow before gaining the glacier. Nearby Dragon Peak (D) is to the right.

Nearing the summit of Catacombs Mountain, the route curves around the closest false summit, ascending a slope out of view here.

Descending from Catacombs Mountain to the alpine valley below. Fortress Mountain is on the right.

Difficulty:
difficult scramble (4th, F)

Hazards:
rockfall; dangerous river
crossings; early-season
avalanches

Round-trip distance:
64 km

Total elevation gain:
2700 m

Round-trip time: 3 days

Recommended seasons:
summer; fall

Maps:
83C12 Athabasca Falls;
83C05 Fortress Lake

*Castle-related nomenclature is common for mountains and this peak is certainly deserving of the name. Its northern, eastern and western sides are quite impenetrable. Thankfully for the peak-bagger, gullies on the southwest face allow for a mostly tame (if treacherously loose!) ascent. Save this for a clear day, as the views are exceptional.*

ACCESS: Via Hwy 93. Park at the Sunwapta Falls trailhead (directly behind the Sunwapta Falls resort) on the west side of the Icefields Parkway 55 km south of Jasper or 98 km north of Saskatchewan Crossing. Follow the signs for Fortress Lake Trail leading southwards from the parking area across a bridge over Sunwapta Falls.

The views of Fortress Lake itself make the lengthy approach worthwhile.

Below: the route ascends the southwest face of Fortress Mountain (F) by means of the large (and loose) gully as seen from the summit of Mount Clemenceau. Also visible are Catacombs Mountain (C), Mount Warren (W) and Mount Brazeau (B).

APPROACH: Via Fortress Lake Trail. Follow the description given for Catacombs Mountain on p158 until you cross the Athabasca River. Once across the river, follow the old Fortress Lake trail (expect significant deadfall and debris due to the lack of trail maintenance) as it winds across the low forest dividing the Athabasca and Chaba rivers. The trail winds 6 km through bush before reaching the bank of the Chaba. Crossing the Chaba should only be attempted at low water, such as in the morning during the fall, and it can be exceptionally dangerous during the spring melt. If conditions are favourable, cross the river by intersecting several sandbanks, trending southwestward to the western shore (look for a yellow marker on the far side of the river that signs the trail). Once across the river you are a mere 1.5 km from the BC border and the edge of Hamber Provincial Park. There are two likely official campsites for ascending Fortress Mountain: on the far east side of the lake at GR 514012; or 2.7 km along the north shore (recommended by the authors) beside the outlet of Fortress Creek at GR 495018.

From the campsite, bushwhack up Fortress Creek. The terrain on the climber's right (east) side of the creek is slightly more pleasant, but still be prepared for a character-building ascent. Ascend the creek for 3 km (and 600 metres of vertical) before reaching a rockbed that marks the start of the ascent gully (at GR 494046). From here the route follows first up grassy ledges which then give way to exceptionally loose scree tunnels. The authors agreed this was the loosest mountain they had ever been on, so be mindful of rockfall on anyone below. Follow the largest gully system as it winds upwards some 600 m from the end of the grassy slopes until it tops out near the summit ridge. You can either directly reach the summit ridge (difficult scrambling but very loose and moderately exposed), or stick slightly lower and traverse loose rubble-strewn ledges eastwards to the summit. Once you are on the summit ridge, the terrain mellows and the ridge can be easily scrambled to the summit. Be mindful of the glacier on the north side of the summit ridge. On descent the lower (traverse) line is advised, to avoid downclimbing the loose and exposed scrambling terrain. Once back down beside the creek, retrace your steps to the campground. A dip in the lake at the end of the trip is quite refreshing and highly recommended!

Difficulty:
easy scramble (3rd, F)

Hazards:
rockfall; early-season
avalanches

Round-trip distance:
22 km

Total elevation gain:
1750 m

Round-trip time:
13–15 hours

Recommended seasons:
summer; fall; winter (skis)

ATES rating:
complex

Map:
83C12 Athabasca Falls

*While certainly less popular than peaks to the northeast on the Skyline trail, Evelyn Peak offers peakbaggers great views of 11,000ers such as Mount Edith Cavell and Mount Fryatt and also a front-seat view of the glaciated northeast face of Mount Kerkeslin. Be prepared for a bit of a bushwhacking on the approach trail.*

ACCESS: Via Hwy 93, 23 km south of Jasper or 127 km north of Saskatchewan Crossing. The parking area is on the east side of the highway near the outlet of a small creek.

APPROACH: From the road there is an old trail (with some recent flagging) that leads up towards "Evelyn Lake." To reach the trail, leave the southeast side of the parking area (passing by several large boulders preventing further vehicle traffic) before cutting south through an open section. Look for orange and pink flagging tape and blazes on nearby trees. After 1.5 km the trail winds beside the roaring waters of Evelyn Creek. At the 3 km mark you will come across an old bridge allowing passage across Evelyn Creek; this marks the end of the bush-free section of the trail. From here things become much more overgrown but the trail trench is still quite visible (with the odd piece of flagging to further aid progress). It is 3 km past the bridge before the trail leaves the bush to enter a broad boulder field. Aim southeast through the boulder field, and before long you will reach the north shore of "Evelyn Lake." The lake can be traversed on the east shore until reaching the base of a prominent gully at GR 470343 which marks the start of the ascent route.

From the north shore of "Evelyn Lake," ascend a prominent slabby gully for 600 vertical metres. It is generally preferable to stick on the climber's left (northwest) side and cross over to climber's right only once near the top when a large cliffband blocks further passage. Once above the cliffband, trend upwards to climber's left for 300 vertical metres to intersect a rib coming off from the summit ridge. Follow this rib upwards, and once on the summit ridge head north to the true summit on easy scrambling terrain. During the ascent it may look like the south summit is higher, but rest assured that once on the true summit you can (just barely) see over the southern peak. Step carefully on your way down the main gully, as the slabs can be quite slick. If planning to split the ascent into two days, overnighting at the lake makes for a very pleasant outing (confirm with Parks in Jasper to secure a backcountry camping permit first).

Great views of the glacier on Mount Kerkeslin (K) across the valley. "Evelyn Lake" is visible below, while Mount Bras Croche (B) looms in the left background.

Difficulty:
easy scramble (3rd, F)

Hazards:
rockfall; early-season avalanches

Round-trip distance:
14 km

Total elevation gain:
1500 m

Round-trip time:
7–9 hours

Recommended seasons:
summer; fall; winter (snowshoes)

ATES rating:
challenging

Map:
83C12 Athabasca Falls

*An excellent viewpoint with a fairly short approach, Mount Hardisty is serendipitously situated to allow for views down the Icefields Parkway and over the Tonquin Valley, as well as towards the Skyline Trail. While the approach can be quite bushy, the upper slopes are straightforward and can also be ascended in winter.*

ACCESS: Via Hwy 93, 23 km south of Jasper or 127 km north of Saskatchewan Crossing. Parking is on the east side of the highway near the outlet of a small creek.

APPROACH: From the road there is an old trail that heads up the north side of Evelyn Creek (which is shared with the approach route for nearby Evelyn Peak). Start by leaving the southeast side of the parking area (passing by several large boulders limiting vehicle traffic) before cutting south through an open section. Look for orange and pink flagging tape and blazes

The route up Mount Hardisty follows the skyline ridge to the summit as seen here from Evelyn Peak.

on nearby trees. After 1.5 km the trail winds beside the roaring waters of Evelyn Creek and passes by the gentlest part of the ridge descending from Mount Hardisty. An ascent of Mount Hardisty should leave the trail near here.

When leaving the trail, aim for a line trending northeast, gaining elevation through initial dense bush which starts to open up as you ascend higher. From the trail it is a little over 2 km of distance and 700 metres of elevation to reach treeline, so long as you stick near the crest of the ridge and don't go too far to the eastern side. Once at treeline, work your way up a large boulder field before reaching the first of two false summits. Carry on scrambling near the ridgecrest over the false summits until the true summit presents itself. In winter the ridge can be corniced, and descending slightly onto the steep east face may be required (be careful to assess the stability of this slope before committing to it). Descend along the same route, and resist the temptation to cut back to the road too early or you will face technical cliffbands.

The view south towards Mount Kerkeslin may be the highlight of this ascent.

Difficulty:
moderate scramble (3rd, F)

Hazards:
rockfall; early-season
avalanches

Round-trip distance:
17 km

Total elevation gain:
1650 m

Round-trip time:
11–14 hours

Recommended seasons:
summer; fall

Map:
83C12 Athabasca Falls

*A peak of many names, "Geraldine Peak," otherwise referred to as Whirlpool Mountain or Pleated Peak, is home to many ascents, including an alpine rock route as well as the moderate scrambling line described here.*

ACCESS: Via the Geraldine fire road. From Jasper head south down Hwy 93 for 27 km until you reach the junction at Athabasca Falls. Turn right onto Hwy 93A and carry on for a little over 1 km before reaching the start of the Geraldine fire road on your left. Follow the road for 6 km to the signed trailhead.

Looking up towards Geraldine Peak (G) from the upper Geraldine Lakes valley with the campsite (C) also shown. Photo: Eric Coulthard.

APPROACH: From the end of the road, follow the Geraldine Lakes trail. This track has a fearsome reputation among hikers (complete with oodles of rock hopping, countless tree roots, and slimy sections), but to the seasoned peakbagger with sturdy boots this is just another day in the hills. Follow the trail as it winds to the first Geraldine Lake (around 2 km from trailhead), and then carry on through slopes laden with avalanche debris before passing the second Geraldine Lake (more of a pond, given its size). From here the trail winds upwards through a sea of downed trees to climber's left of the headwall, ascending scree to reach the third lake.

From the third lake, carry on along the trail (hopping over the many boulders that line the route) until you make your way to the cozy and scenic Geraldine Lakes campground (a great place to stay if splitting the ascent over two days). Leave the campground by following the shoreline westwards to the base of the peak where the bush gives way to scree slopes (some 400 m from the campground). Start your ascent on the climber's right (north) side of the bush, ascending scree and talus. Carry on upwards until you reach the ridgecrest, and then continue upwards, trending toward climber's left and hopping up boulders. About 200 vertical metres up the ridge you will encounter some large slabs forcing you to climber's right (back onto the ridgecrest). From here, we recommend you stick close to the crest for the next 300 vertical metres until the false summit is reached. Once you are atop the ridge, getting to the true summit involves a short, moderate downclimb and a traverse through a snow slope that is persistent in all but the driest of years (if the snow is hard here, a mountaineering axe can be very advantageous). From the true summit, the next visible high point is crowned with a large cairn. Despite appearances this is not the summit but instead the top of the (much more frequented) alpine route. Reaching this summit is possible but requires downclimbing difficult scrambling terrain and should only be attempted in good conditions.

# MOUNT FRYATT (SOUTHWEST FACE), 3361 M ☐

Difficulty:
alpine climb (5.4, PD)

Hazards:
rockfall; early-season
avalanches

Round-trip distance:
32 km

Total elevation gain:
2300 m

Round-trip time:
2- 3 days

Recommended seasons·
summer; fall

Map:
83C12 Athabasca Falls

*Named for Charles Fryatt, captain of the merchant ship* Brussels *(which name itself graces nearby Brussels Peak), who achieved celebrity status in the First World War by taunting German U-boats.*

ACCESS: Via the Geraldine fire road. From Jasper head south down Hwy 93 for 27 km until you reach the junction for Athabasca Falls. Turn right onto Hwy 93A and carry on for a little over 1 km before reaching the start of the Geraldine fire road on your left. Follow the road for 6 km to the signed trailhead.

Ascending Mount Fryatt (F) via the southwest face requires traversing alpine meadows and steep scree before reaching the bivy site (B) and then the start of the technical climbing. Photo: David P. Jones.

APPROACH: Follow the approach directions for Geraldine Peak on p169 until you reach the north shore of the third Geraldine Lake. Stick on the trail as it winds above the eastern side of the lake. The official campground on the south side of the lake makes for a good place to overnight if splitting the approach into two days. Carry on along the trail as it passes along the western shores of a duo of lakes. Past the second lake the trail becomes faint as you enter alpine meadows. Carry on to an open slope around GR 350231. From here, head east up the valley, sidehilling above yet another unnamed lake to the south as you work your way towards the base of Mount Fryatt's southwest face. Expect some challenges while sidehilling. Around GR 375214, you'll reach "Iceberg Lake," the north shore of which makes for an excellent bivy site. Allow 6–8 hours to cover the 13 km of distance and 1300 metres of elevation gain from the road.

Good climbing higher up on the southwest face of Mount Fryatt. Photo: Eric Coulthard.

From the bivy site at "Iceberg Lake," there is still 840 vertical metres of elevation to the summit. Start by crossing to the eastern side of the lake and angle upward to climber's right to reach a break in the cliffband above. Once past the cliffband, traverse back to climber's left across the face until you come to one of several couloirs leading upwards (which are often icy even late into the summer). Carry on upwards for 400 vertical metres along a mixture of scrambling terrain and technical climbing (up to 5.4 with good route-finding) until you reach the west ridge at a high bench. From here, carrying on up the west ridge is quite technical. Instead, traverse the face on exposed and steep scree to reach the south ridge, which you can then scramble up to the summit.

Difficulty:
mountaineering (glacier
travel; 4th, PD)

Hazards:
rockfall; crevasses;
avalanches

Round-trip distance:
12 km

Total elevation gain:
1750 m

Round-trip time:
7–12 hours

Recommended seasons:
summer; fall; winter (skis)

ATES rating:
complex

Map:
83C06 Sunwapta Peak

*Translated from Stoney Nakoda as "turbulent river," Sunwapta is home to two ascent routes: a river of ice on the north aspect (described here), and a river of scree on the southwest. The north glacier is an aesthetic line through big terrain that is not to be underestimated but makes for a good day out.*

ACCESS: Via Hwy 93. Park roadside on the north bank of Grizzly Creek at GR 764005, 85 km south of Jasper or 68 km north of Saskatchewan Crossing.

APPROACH: From the road, set out into the bush heading upstream. Follow the creek for 2 km, gaining 450 metres of elevation to reach treeline. Carry on up the valley, following the low point as you curve towards the lower glacier.

The north glacier of Sunwapta Mountain makes for an impressive sight. The route here follows up the valley before ascending the crevassed upper glacier and gaining the summit ridge.

The ascent route first gains elevation in the upper valley on scree before intercepting the glacier and heading upwards. Photo: Eric Coulthard.

As you ascend the valley, aim for the tongue of the lower glacier on the climber's right (southern) side of the slope, crossing a gently glaciated bench that leads to the first major icefall. Reach the upper glacier by ascending the gentlest line on climber's right (see the "upper glacier" image above), then traverse a bench to climber's left to gain the glaciated north ridge. From here continue ascending the ridge until you reach the broad upper glacier. Your route to the summit will depend considerably on the glacial coverage and can range from a simple walk to a complex crevasse maze. Your aim will be to work your way to climber's right to gain the west ridge. Once on the ridge, a short glacial hike will let you top out onto the summit. On descent, it is recommended to follow the scramble route (described next, on p175).

Difficulty:
easy scramble (2nd, F)

Hazards:
rockfall

Round-trip distance:
10 km

Total elevation gain:
1740 m

Round-trip time:
8–12 hours

Recommended seasons:
summer; fall

Map:
83C06 Sunwapta Peak

*There are few routes that offer better views without tramping over technical terrain than the southwest face of Sunwapta Peak. While only an easy scramble, this route ascends to nearly 11,000er elevation and is well located to descry many of those elusive peaks. Come mentally prepared for a long day of working your way up the seemingly endless slope. And be sure to bring extra batteries for your camera!*

ACCESS: Via Hwy 93. Park on the east side of the road at the sign for the Stanley Falls hiking trail 88 km south of Jasper (and 2 km south of the Beauty Creek hostel) or 65 km north of Saskatchewan Crossing.

APPROACH: The route begins directly from the side of the road and ascends to the north of the prominent drainage above.

The scramble route up Sunwapta Peak (S) is a long but straightforward plod.

ICEFIELDS PARKWAY SUNWAPTA PEAK (SOUTHWEST FACE)

The broad scree slopes on Sunwapta Peak do not have much variety. An ascent party can be seen in the top right of the image. Photo: Eric Coulthard.

From the side of the road, follow an obvious trail on the north side of the drainage as it winds upwards. From the start of the route, there is 2.5 km of distance and 700 metres of elevation to reach treeline. While the rubbly scramble to the summit may not look very demanding from the road, after treeline there is still 1000 vertical metres to be gained. After reaching treeline, trend slightly to climber's right, sticking in the middle of the broad scree slopes, and plod your way upwards. Be sure to take plenty of breaks to appreciate the slowly unfolding views all around. Due to the height of this peak, snow can linger on its upper reaches into early summer. If in doubt, a mountaineering axe may be useful for the upper slopes. Reaching the summit, your perseverance is rewarded with possibly the best view for the effort in Jasper National Park.

Difficulty:
off-trail hike (2nd, F)

Hazards:
rockfall

Round-trip distance:
11 km

Total elevation gain:
1200 m

Round-trip time:
4–6 hours

Recommended seasons:
summer; fall

Map:
83C06 Sunwapta Peak

*Possibly one of the best views in Jasper National Park for the effort expended. An ascent of Tangle Ridge is highly recommended for a peakbagger looking for a short day.*

ACCESS: Via Hwy 93, 96 km south of Jasper or 57 km north of Saskatchewan Crossing. The parking area is on the west side of the highway, beside Tangle Falls.

APPROACH: From the parking lot, cross to the east side of the road and continue upwards for 500 m to reach the start of the signed Wilcox Pass Trail. Follow this official trail for 1.6 km until you reach a creek draining from farther up the valley.

Stay on the west side of the creek as you head upwards (looking for cairns). After 300 vertical metres you reach treeline and the views really start to open up. From treeline, trend slightly climber's left on the gradual slope and work your way towards the summit. The summit ridge is adorned with a well-equipped radio repeater.

Looking towards Tangle Ridge (T) from low on the ridge below Mount Kitchener. Sunwapta Peak (S) and the col that leads to Beauty Lakes (B) are also visible.

Tangle Ridge is an excellent viewpoint for peaks to the east of the Columbia Icefield, including Mount Andromeda (centre), Mount Athabasca (centre left) and Wilcox Peak (left).

Difficulty:
easy scramble (3rd, F)

Hazards:
rockfall; early-season
avalanches

Round-trip distance:
21 km

Total elevation gain:
2000 m

Round-trip time:
11–13 hours

Recommended seasons:
summer; fall; winter (skis)

ATES rating:
challenging

Map:
83C06 Sunwapta Peak

*An unofficial name for one of the summits towering above Beauty Lakes, "Chilly Peak" is guarded by cliffs and glaciers on its eastern aspect but can be easily ascended on its south-west slopes. While it used to be possible to camp in the Beauty Lakes area, Parks has been less than forthcoming with backcountry permits for the place recently. If legally allowed, a camp beside the lakes and an ascent of "Chilly Peak" makes for a lovely overnight outing.*

ACCESS: Via Hwy 93, 96 km south of Jasper or 57 km north of Saskatchewan Crossing. The parking area is on the west side of the highway, beside Tangle Falls.

APPROACH: From the parking lot, cross to the east side of the road and continue upwards for 500 m to reach the start of the signed Wilcox Pass Trail. Follow this official trail for just under 2 km before branching off and aiming northeast to the saddle (near GR 836928; see the image on p177) descending from the east ridge of Tangle Ridge. The saddle sits at 2670 metres and is a good viewpoint for the surrounding valley. Descend from the saddle by making a straight line northwards through rubbly rock and into alpine meadows, reaching Beauty Lakes after 4 km.

From the lakes, continue northwards through the valley. "Chilly Peak" is directly ahead, and while a frontal assault would be quite slabby and unpleasant, walking farther along to the south ridge allows for a gentle scree ramble upwards. Stick near the crest of the ridge for the 400 metres of elevation between the valley and the summit. In early season conditions, be wary of cornices on the summit ridge. Retrace your steps on the way down.

POSSIBLE EXTENSION: While in the area, wandering up "The Claw" is a short diversion with slightly different views. See p180 for route details.

An easy walk up Chilly Peak (C) as seen from the valley beside Beauty Lake.
Photo: Eric Coulthard.

Difficulty:
moderate scramble (3rd, F)

Hazards:
rockfall; early-season
avalanches

Round-trip distance:
16 km

Total elevation gain:
1900 m

Round-trip time:
8–11 hours

Recommended seasons:
summer; fall

Map:
83C06 Sunwapta Peak

*"The Claw" is an unofficial name for a talon of rock jutting up above Beauty Lakes. While not a serious ascent, "The Claw" can grant excellent views for the small detour needed to climb it if a peakbagger happens to be in the area. As for nearby "Chilly Peak," obtaining an overnight permit from Parks for camping at Beauty Lakes can be difficult, but if achieved it makes for a good overnight outing.*

ACCESS: Via Hwy 93, 96 km south of Jasper or 57 km north of Saskatchewan Crossing. The parking area is on the west side of the highway, beside Tangle Falls.

APPROACH: Follow the approach to Beauty Lakes described for "Chilly Peak" on p178.

Beauty Lakes is a very aesthetic area. Photo: Eric Coulthard.

Once you are at Beauty Lakes, The Claw is directly visible on climber's right. Carry on northwards, crossing a second large lake, and then directly ascend the scree slope leading towards the summit. Follow the scree until you reach the summit ridge, then trend to climber's left for the last 50 vertical metres. Watch out for patches of slab near the summit which can be exceptionally slippery when wet.

POSSIBLE EXTENSION: After making the approach into Beauty Lakes, carrying on northwards and ascending "Chilly Peak" makes for a good full day if you've got extra energy.

Opposite page: Ascending The Claw (C) is a short side trip but worthwhile if you're in the Beauty Lakes area (especially as a vantage point for sunrise and sunset). Photo: Eric Coulthard.

Difficulty:
mountaineering (glacier
travel; steep snow; 4th, PD)

Hazards:
rockfall; river crossings;
glacier travel; serac fall;
avalanches

Round-trip distance:
9 km
(from Woolley Creek bivy)

Total elevation gain:
1250 m
(from Woolley Creek bivy)

Round-trip time:
7–9 hours
(from Woolley Creek bivy)

Recommended seasons:
late summer; fall

Map:
83C06 Sunwapta Peak

*A popular route on an aesthetic peak, Mount Woolley offers views from both the summit and the bivy site that make this a must-do on any peakbagger's list. Wait until later in the season for rockfall in the ascent gullies to diminish. Do not underestimate the hazard of the glacier crossing, either: while relatively short, it harbours many holes as well as overhead serac danger.*

ACCESS: Via Hwy 93. Park on the east side of the highway at an unsigned pullout beneath the northern end of Tangle Peak. The parking area is 91 km south of Jasper or 62 km north of Saskatchewan Crossing, at GR 775945.

APPROACH: The described routes for Mount Woolley, Diadem Peak, Mushroom Peak and Little Alberta all share the same approach via Woolley Creek. This approach starts from the highway and first involves crossing the braided Sunwapta River. This crossing can be a serious undertaking, and often this stream is not traversable until August when meltwater has decreased. Even during traditionally low-melt months, it is a good idea to cross early in the morning to further reduce hazard. Aim to reach the west bank just before the outlet of Woolley Creek (the first gully visible from the parking lot). On the south side of the creek a good trail leads upwards into the bush for a little under 1 km before opening up into a mixture of rock and mud

The route to reach the Woolley/Diadem col (C) requires travelling across a broken glacier, ascending steep snow and traversing loose rock slopes. It is not to be underestimated.

that travels beside the creek. Carry on alongside the creek for 2 km until you reach an improvised log bridge where the trail crosses to the north side and travels through a large boulder field. There are many possible paths through the boulders, but sticking to the north side of the valley (look for numerous cairns) is the most efficient line. Past the boulders, the trail winds steeply upwards on the west side of the creek, eventually coming to the Woolley Creek bivy site at 2285 m (GR 726939) just south of a glacial lake. The bivy site has gathered a number of substantial corrals over the years for wind shelters and makes for a fine camp when bagging the surrounding peaks. The total distance to the bivy site is 6.5 km with 700 metres of elevation gain. Allow 4–6 hours to make the trip in.

From the bivy site, pass the west side of the glacial lake and cross the inflowing runoff stream from Woolley/Diadem Glacier. Ascend the lower glacier, working your way around large crevasses and aiming for the wide gully to climber's right of Diadem Peak. This gully can be a fearsome rock chute, so time your ascent to avoid periods of intense rockfall. Kick steps up the lower section of the gully until you reach a gap (see routeline image on p183) that allows for passage onto the ledge system on climber's left. Ascend the ledges (which can be exceptionally tricky if wet or icy), trending upwards to climber's left to intersect the higher gully (look for cairns marking where to leave the ledges). Once in the second gully, kick steps upwards until you reach a bench on your left that allows for access to easier terrain. The consequences of a slip in this gully would be considerable, and most parties would benefit from an anchored belay. Stay vigilant on the upper glacier: there are still numerous crevasses to be found. Stick to the northern edge of the slope on scree where possible (see the routeline image for Diadem Peak, p186). With a few minutes of plodding you will reach the Woolley/Diadem col (itself with an impressive elevation of 3200 m). From the col, carry on upwards, avoiding crevasses by staying in the middle of the slope, and ascend a broad bump before the final summit ridge presents itself. Often a steep, exposed snow step is the final obstacle to reach the summit (see photo of the summit ridge of Mount Woolley on p185).

POSSIBLE EXTENSION: An ascent of Mount Woolley is ideally combined with nearby Diadem Peak. See Diadem Peak at p187 for the route description from the Woolley/Diadem col. Add 2 hours to ascend Diadem Peak and return to the Woolley/Diadem col.

The aesthetic summit ridge of Mount Woolley has one steep snow slope but is otherwise straightforward if you follow near the ridgecrest, being wary of cornices.

# DIADEM PEAK, 3375 M

□

Difficulty:
mountaineering (glacier
travel; steep snow; 4th, PD)

Hazards:
rockfall; river crossings;
glacier travel; serac fall;
avalanches

Round-trip distance:
8 km
(from Woolley Creek bivy)

Total elevation gain:
1200 m
(from Woolley Creek bivy)

Round-trip time:
7–9 hours
(from Woolley Creek bivy)

Recommended seasons:
late summer; fall

Map:
83C06 Sunwapta Peak

*Like the jewellery it is named for, Diadem Peak is crowned with a picturesque snowfield that radiantly glistens by sun or moon. While the "diadem" can be reached by a straightforward line from the Woolley/Diadem col, the true summit requires a short, exposed technical step.*

ACCESS: Via Hwy 93. Park on the east side of the highway at an unsigned pullout beneath the northern end of Tangle Ridge. The parking area is 91 km south of Jasper or 62 km north of Saskatchewan Crossing, at GR 775945.

APPROACH: The described routes for Mount Woolley, Diadem Peak, Mushroom Peak and Little Alberta all share the same approach to the Woolley Creek bivy site. See p182 for details about the approach. Allow 4–6 hours to reach the bivy site from the highway.

From the Woolley/Diadem col (C) the route scrambles up the ridge before traversing a snowy scree slope towards the summit. The false (but more popular) summit (F) is visible, with the true summit out of view farther along the ridge.

ICEFIELDS PARKWAY DIADEM PEAK

Traversing from the false summit to the true one. The route aims for the left side of the rock pinnacle and then traverses the gully (G) to the true summit (D). Photo: Vern Dewit.

Diadem Peak shares the same ascent route as Mount Woolley until you reach the Woolley/Diadem col. See the Mount Woolley route description at p184 for details. From the col, ascend the south-facing rock ridge for 150 vertical metres before reaching the summit scree/snow slope. Follow the slope upwards to its high point, staying well clear of cornices on the eastern side. To reach the true summit, lose a small amount of elevation as you continue along the ridge, aiming for a rock pinnacle with a short gully leading to the true summit (see "false summit" image above). Gain the pinnacle on its north side and then work your way around it, traversing a steep snow/rock step followed by a few moderate scrambling moves to reach the summit. Many parties may appreciate a belay for this final section. Retrace your steps on return, being mindful of the time of day; snow bridges may lose stability and considerable rockfall can rain down the ascent gullies.

POSSIBLE EXTENSION: Diadem Peak can often be combined with an ascent of Mount Woolley. See p184 for route details from the Woolley/Diadem col. Add 2 hours to ascend Woolley and get back to the Woolley/Diadem col.

The true summit of Diadem Peak (some 5 m above the snowy summit as measured with a barometric altimeter) is reached via a short steep rock section with considerable exposure on the eastern face.

Difficulty:
moderate scramble (3rd, F)

Hazards:
rockfall; early-season
avalanches

Round-trip distance:
6.4 km
(from Woolley Creek bivy)

Total elevation gain:
950 m
(from Woolley Creek bivy)

Round-trip time:
5–8 hours
(from Woolley Creek bivy)

Recommended seasons:
summer; fall

Map:
83C06 Sunwapta Peak

*The least technical peak accessed from the Woolley Creek bivy site, Mushroom Peak is named for the curious rock formations that adorn the slopes near the summit. With careful route-finding Mushroom can be reached without glacier travel and is a worthy backup if conditions are unfavourable for other ascents in the area.*

ACCESS: Via Hwy 93. Park on the east side of the highway at an unsigned pullout beneath the northern end of Tangle Ridge. The parking area is located 91 km south of Jasper or 62 km north of Saskatchewan Crossing, at GR 775945.

APPROACH: The described routes for Mount Woolley, Diadem Peak, Mushroom Peak and Little Alberta all share the same approach to the Woolley Creek bivy site. See p182 for details about the approach. Allow 4–6 hours to reach the bivy site from the highway.

Leaving the bivy site, pass the west side of the lake, crossing over several mounds of scree and aiming for the edge of Diadem Glacier as it nears the slopes of Mushroom Peak. To avoid travelling on the glacier, stick climber's right and ascend until directly beneath steep, south-facing cliff-bands. From here, head climber's left (west), traversing rocky ledges and passing beneath a drainage that often forms a waterfall. Once above the glacier, work your way farther north, ascending on the rubbly slopes of Mushroom's west face. While many lines are possible to reach the summit, sticking close to the western ridge ensures the most efficient rock for ascending. Near the summit the interesting rock formations that gave the peak its name can be seen. The final summit cairn is then reached with a few moderate moves. Descend the same way you came, being careful to remember the correct path to weave through the lower rock band

Looking over from the slopes near Woolley's shoulder towards Woolley/Diadem col (C), Mushroom Peak (M) and the bivy site (B).

Difficulty:
mountaineering (brief
glacier travel; 3rd, F)

Hazards:
rockfall; river crossing;
crevasses; avalanches

Round-trip distance:
9 km
(from Lloyd MacKay Hut)

Total elevation gain:
950 m
(from Lloyd MacKay Hut)

Round-trip time:
4–6 hours
(from Lloyd MacKay Hut)

Recommended seasons:
summer; fall

Map:
83C06 Sunwapta Peak

*Even at almost 3000 metres elevation, this is only a "little" mountain, given its neighbours The Twins, Mounts Columbia and Woolley and of course the fearsome Mount Alberta. Still, Little Alberta is an outstanding viewpoint and certainly worth ascending if you're in the area. Take note that the statistics above do not include the lengthy approach to Lloyd MacKay Hut, described below.*

ACCESS: Via Hwy 93. Park on the east side of the highway at an unsigned pullout beneath the northern end of Tangle Ridge. The parking area is located 91 km south of Jasper or 62 km north of Saskatchewan Crossing at GR 775945.

APPROACH: The described routes for Mount Woolley, Diadem Peak, Mushroom Peak and Little Alberta all share the same approach to the Woolley Creek bivy site. See p182 for details about the approach. Allow 4–6 hours to reach the bivy site from the highway. While Little Alberta can be ascended from the bivy in a day, the authors recommend pushing on to Lloyd MacKay Hut and overnighting there for the lovely views it provides.

From the Woolley Creek bivy site, head southwest, ascending loose rock to gain a gentle rock ridge. Above the ridge a higher glacial lake is visible with reflections of Mount Engelhard looming above. Pass the lake on its west side, following near the southwest face of Mount Woolley as you

The route up Woolley's Shoulder is very loose and treacherous, especially with lingering snow. Photo: Vern Dewit.

round the bend facing up a steep, loose gully. The next 400 vertical metres to reach the top of the gully (called Woolley's Shoulder) are very character-building given the astonishingly loose rock. This section can be quite dangerous in wet conditions. Take heart, though: after running this gauntlet you are rewarded with one of the best views in the Rockies. After admiring the sights, descend the west face of the shoulder on scree, traversing towards the northern end of Little Alberta. The route briefly steps onto the edge of the glacier descending from Mount Woolley's south face, so be sure to take appropriate precautions. Lloyd MacKay Hut is perched at an elevation of 2720 metres (GR 700930), and what it lacks in luxury it more than makes up for in ambience. Allow 7–9 hours to reach the hut from the road (a distance of 11 km and 1400 m of elevation gain).

Ascending Little Alberta requires reaching a break in the cliffbands near the south side of the peak. Leave the hut and head south, descending a wide (and often wet) scree/boulder ramp paralleling the steep cliffs on the west face of Little Alberta. After losing around 300 metres of elevation, the terrain flattens out and travel becomes straightforward as you work your way around the far side of the peak. After you've travelled around 2 km from the hut, the cliffs start to shorten eventually, revealing a series of loose ledges on climber's left that can be traversed to get onto the peak's south face. Continue traversing the south face for 500 m until the cliffbands above give way to gentler scree slopes. Ascend the scree for 300 vertical metres to the gentle, south-facing summit ridge. From here follow the ridge upwards to the cairned summit. Be sure to bring extra batteries for your camera, as the views from the summit are extraordinary.

From Lloyd MacKay Hut (LM) the route up Little Alberta (LA) traverses the entire west face before reaching a break in the cliffbands. Mount Woolley (W) is visible at left, while the Stutfield Peaks loom on the right.

LA

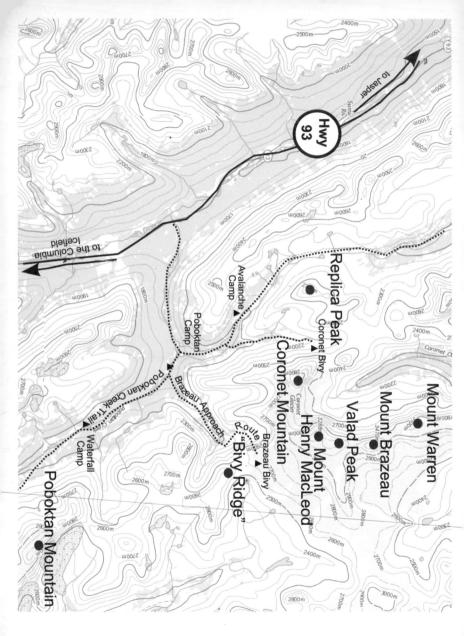

to Jasper

Hwy 93

to the Columbia Icefield

Avalanche Camp

Poboktan Camp

Poboktan Creek Trail

Brazeau Approach

Waterfall Camp

Poboktan Mountain

Replica Peak

Coronet Bivy

Coronet Mountain

Coronet Glacier

Route

Brazeau Bivy

"Bivy Ridge"

Mount Henry MacLeod

Valad Peak

Mount Brazeau

Mount Warren

# LE GRAND BRAZEAU

| MOUNTAIN | ELEVATION (M) | ROUTE TYPE | PAGE |
|---|---|---|---|
| Coronet Mountain | 3152 | Mountaineering | 200 |
| Mount Brazeau | 3470 | Mountaineering | 202 |
| Mount Henry MacLeod | 3307 | Mountaineering | 206 |
| Valad Peak | 3250 | Mountaineering | 208 |
| Mount Warren | 3362 | Mountaineering | 210 |
| "Bivy Ridge" (GR 780175) | 2766 | Easy scramble | 212 |
| Poboktan Mountain | 3322 | Easy scramble | 214 |
| Replica Peak | 2794 | Easy scramble | 216 |

## AREA OVERVIEW

Le Grand Brazeau is the name of the range of mountains that bridge the southern end of Maligne Lake to the northern end of Brazeau Lake. This in an impressive array of peaks, including two 11,000ers (Mounts Brazeau and Warren), as well as numerous other glaciated peaks with technical and non-technical ascent lines. For peakbaggers comfortable with glacier travel, the peaks on the Brazeau Icefield are sure to be alluring. For those averse to glacier travel, the non-glaciated scrambles in this chapter grant views almost as impressive and with limited hazards.

## ACCESS, ACCOMMODATIONS AND FACILITIES

The most reasonable way to access this region is via Hwy 93, the Icefields Parkway, either from Jasper to the north or Saskatchewan Crossing from the south. All of the peaks described here are can also be accessed via the Poboktan Creek trailhead, which lies 72 km south of Jasper or 81 km north of Saskatchewan Crossing. It is also possible to access the peaks on the Brazeau Icefield from the north by canoeing across Maligne Lake, but this approach is not described here (see Bill Corbett's *The 11,000ers of The Canadian Rockies* for a description of this approach).

There are no restaurants, backcountry lodges or outfitters in this region, so all food and logistical supplies should be purchased elsewhere before setting off. There are three official Parks Canada campgrounds described in this region, all of which can be reserved by contacting the information centre in Jasper or https://reservation.pc.gc.ca/Jasper.

## PERMITS AND RESTRICTIONS

All of the trips in this section lie within Jasper National Park and thus are subject to restrictions. Obtain more information from Parks Canada in Jasper or on the Parks Canada website for current policies on camping and backcountry travel. Many of the routes described here require bivouacs, which in turn require backcountry random camping permits. These too can be obtained from the information centre in Jasper. Lastly, overnight human traffic in the Maligne Pass area (near the described route for Replica Peak) is additionally restricted by a quota system. Contact Parks for details on availability of reservations for the Avalanche campground.

Below: the peaks of the Brazeau Icefield as seen from the summit of Poboktan Mountain: Coronet Mountain (C), Mount Henry MacLeod (HM), Valad Peak (V), Mount Warren (W), Mount Brazeau (B), Bivy Ridge (BR) and the Brazeau bivy site (BV) are shown. Photo: Vern Dewit.

## CORONET MOUNTAIN, 3152 M ☐

**Difficulty:**
mountaineering (glacier travel; steep snow; 4th, PD−)

**Hazards:**
rockfall; crevasses; avalanches

**Round-trip distance:**
29 km

**Total elevation gain:**
1600 m

**Round-trip time:**
2–3 days

**Recommended seasons:**
summer; fall

**Maps:**
83C06 Sunwapta Peak; 83C11 Southesk Lake

*Like nearby Replica Peak, Coronet Mountain was named by Harold Palmer in 1923. A coronet is a type of ceremonial headdress which Palmer thought described the snowcap that crowns the summit.*

ACCESS: Via Hwy 93, 72 km south of Jasper or 81 km north of Saskatchewan Crossing. Park on the east side of the highway, on the south side of Poboktan Creek. The trail starts on the north side of the creek, beside the Poboktan warden station (walk across the bridge from the parking area to access it).

APPROACH: Depart from the warden station on the signed Poboktan Creek trail, heading eastwards. Follow the trail for 6 km until you reach an unsigned junction with a trail heading northwards. This branch eventually leads to Maligne Pass. Follow the Maligne Pass trail for 2 km until around GR 740151, where the trail will bend to the west. Here the ascent route for Coronet Mountain leaves the trail and continues north up the valley. Bushwhack in the valley bottom for 2.5 km until you come to rubbly fields of avalanche debris. Carry on up towards the head of the valley to reach open alpine terrain around GR 724188. If you are splitting the trip into two days, this makes a good place for a bivy.

From the bivy the west face of Coronet Mountain looms directly above. The ascent line forms a rising traverse that trends to climber's right on steep scree (and often snow) slopes sticking to climber's right (south) of prominent grey slabs. Carry on upwards for 500 vertical metres until you reach the summit ridge and, shortly after that, a rocky false summit. To reach the true summit, stick to the ridgecrest, following loose, exposed rock, or move onto the glaciated north side of the ridge. A belay to the high point is recommended due to the possibility of a large summit cornice. Descend the same way back to the alpine bivy and then to the road.

Looking up at the west face of Coronet Mountain. The route weaves upwards on scree and snow, avoiding the prominent slabs visible at the centre of the photo. Photo: Steven Song.

Difficulty:
mountaineering (glacier travel; 3rd, PD)

Hazards:
rockfall; crevasses; avalanches

Round-trip distance:
40 km

Total elevation gain:
2300 m

Round-trip time:
2–3 days

Recommended seasons:
summer; fall

Maps:
83C06 Sunwapta Peak; 83C11 Southesk Lake

*Named in 1902 in honour of Joseph Etienne Brazeau, this peak is the highest in the front ranges of the Canadian Rockies and boasts outstanding views. While the ascent slopes of Mount Brazeau are little more than a scramble when dry, there is a considerable amount of glacier travel required to reach the peak. On some older maps in the late 1800s, modern day Mount Brazeau was known as Mount McGillivray after fur trader Duncan McGillivray. In 1957 a less lofty peak in Kananuskis was chosen to bear his name.*

ACCESS: Via Hwy 93, 72 km south of Jasper or 81 km north of Saskatchewan Crossing. Park on the east side of the highway, on the south side of Poboktan Creek. The trail starts on the north side of the creek, beside the warden station (walk across the bridge from the parking area to access it).

A short cliffband can be bypassed by ascending loose scree to reach the final slope to access the bivy site.

The approach valley leading to the Brazeau bivy. The route heads up the valley to a waterfall at the base of the grassy slope on the left.

APPROACH: The approach to Mount Brazeau starts from the warden station and follows the official Poboktan Creek trail for 7 km. Just before leaving the trail you will pass Poboktan Campsite and cross two log bridges. Immediately after the second bridge look for a faint trail branching off to the left (north) side of the trail. While initially somewhat bushy, the trail quickly improves and follows the creek up the valley. The terrain is varied. You will first be moving through several boulder fields before reaching swampy flats at the head of the valley. Cross the flats, aiming for a bubbling waterfall at the north end of the valley. Look for a cairn on the climber's right (east) side of the waterfall. The cairn marks the start of a good trail leading upwards beside the creek. Following this trail as it rises, you will soon start to catch glimpses of glacial ice above! Ascend climber's right to bypass a long grey cliffband on easy scree (see "cliffband" routeline photo on p202). In about 500 m you will reach the start of a large gully of scree-covered, moraine-textured rock. Ascend this gully for 200 vertical metres before topping out and taking in great views of the unnamed peaks to the east (at the headwaters of Brazeau Lake). The recommended bivy site is just ahead at the base of the ridge between you and the lower icefield, at GR 779180. Allow 6–8 hours to reach the bivy site from the highway, covering 14 km and 1300 metres of elevation gain.

Cross the ridge north of the bivy site and drop down the other side to reach the lower glacier. For the upper glacier, aim for the middle of the rocky outcrop to the north (see the routeline on the photo for "Bivy Ridge" on p212).

Once atop the rock section, don your glacier gear and set off upwards to gain the main Brazeau Icefield. There are numerous crevasses around, so stay vigilant with probing. From the base of the upper glacier it is 4 km and 400 vertical metres to the base of Mount Brazeau. Along the way you will pass Mount Henry MacLeod and Valad Peak (both of which can be readily ascended). Aim to leave the icefield by gaining the north ridge that comes down from Valad Peak (at around GR 762213). Once you are on the ridge a short scramble will enable you to cross over to the non-glaciated west face. From there, descend down scree to reach the Valad/Brazeau col. From the col, ascend 400 vertical metres on scree and snow to reach the summit. On descent be wary of snow bridges that may have weakened during the day.

View of the ascent slopes for Mount Brazeau (B) from the Valad/Brazeau col. Mount Mary Vaux (MV) is also visible in the distance.

POSSIBLE EXTENSION: To escalate an ascent of Mount Brazeau into a multi-peak outing, there are several options available. Mount Henry MacLeod and Valad Peak can be ascended fairly easily while en route to the ascent slopes of Brazeau (see p206 and 208 respectively for details). The other 11,000er on the icefield, Mount Warren, can be ascended from the described bivy, but if combined with an ascent of Brazeau it makes more sense to have a high camp on the icefield. See the Mount Warren description on p210 for a suggested route. Lastly, if you have a bit more energy after making it back to the bivy site, a dinnertime ascent of "Bivy Ridge" is a great viewpoint for sunset pictures (see p213).

The summit of Mount Brazeau casts an interesting shadow towards Brazeau Lake at sunset.

**Difficulty:**
mountaineering (glacier travel; 3rd, F)

**Hazards:**
rockfall; crevasses; avalanches

**Round-trip distance:**
8 km
(from Brazeau bivy)

**Total elevation gain:**
500 m
(from Brazeau bivy)

**Round-trip time:**
5–7 hours
(from Brazeau bivy)

**Recommended seasons:**
summer; fall

**Maps:**
83C06 Sunwapta Peak;
83C11 Southesk Lake

*Henry MacLeod was a surveyor for the Canadian Pacific Railway and in 1875 was credited as the first non-Aboriginal to see Maligne Lake. MacLeod originally decided on the name "Sore-Foot Lake" for modern-day Maligne Lake, likely due to unfavourable boots on the journey from the railway.*

ACCESS: Via Hwy 93, 72 km south of Jasper or 81 km north of Saskatchewan Crossing. Park on the east side of the highway, on the south side of Poboktan Creek. The trail starts on the north side of the creek, beside the warden station (walk across the bridge from the parking area to access it).

APPROACH: From the bivy site, follow the ascent route for Mount Brazeau to the middle of the Brazeau Icefield, just over 2 km after gaining the upper glacier (around GR 769204; see the area photo on pp198–99).

Fine views north towards Maligne Lake from the summit of Mount Henry MacLeod. Mount Brazeau (B), Mount Warren (W), Mount Charlton (C) and Mount Unwin (U) are shown.

Near the summit of Mount Henry MacLeod (HM) the route moves off the glacier and onto a rubbly scree ridge to the summit. Photo: Vern Dewit.

Ascend the gentle northeast ridge of the peak, sticking near the crest. Be wary of crevasses along this ridge, especially later in the season. Ascend 250 vertical metres to reach the upper edge of the glacier. The final few vertical meters are gained by scrambling on broken rock to reach the summit plateau.

POSSIBLE EXTENSIONS: From the summit plateau of Mount Henry MacLeod, you can gain nearby Valad Peak by simply descending 150 vertical metres along the intervening north ridge to the MacLeod/Valad col. Stick skier's left (west) to avoid travelling on the glacier. See p208 for the full entry describing Valad Peak. Many parties (especially early in the season) enchain Mount Henry MacLeod, Valad Peak and Mount Brazeau in one loop. The authors recommend ascending Brazeau separately to avoid being on the glacier in the full heat of the afternoon.

Difficulty:
mountaineering (glacier
travel; 3rd, F)

Hazards:
rockfall; crevasses;
avalanches

Round-trip distance:
9 km
(from Brazeau bivy)

Total elevation gain:
450 m
(from Brazeau bivy)

Round-trip time:
5–7 hours
(from Brazeau bivy)

Recommended seasons:
summer; fall

Maps:
83C06 Sunwapta Peak;
83C11 Southesk Lake

*Named for Valad, the Aboriginal guide who travelled with Henry MacLeod in 1875 on his first journey to Maligne Lake. Valad was widely respected in the Jasper region by Aboriginals and Europeans alike.*

ACCESS: Via Hwy 93, 72 km south of Jasper or 81 km north of Saskatchewan Crossing. Park on the east side of the highway, on the south side of Poboktan Creek. The trail starts on the north side of the creek, beside the warden station (walk across the bridge from the parking area to access it).

APPROACH: Follow the approach to the Brazeau Icefield bivy site as described on p203. Allow 6–8 hours to reach the bivy site from the highway.

There are several routes to Valad Peak, and the hazard and difficulty of each will depend on the condition of the glaciers surrounding the peak. The route recommended by the authors involves first ascending the glaciated northeast ridge of Mount Henry MacLeod (see p207). From there, scree slopes on the western face can be reached that will allow for a non-technical traverse down to the MacLeod/Valad col. From the col, ascend scree and a short section of glacier to reach the summit plateau of Valad Peak. Return the way you came, down the gentle northeast ridge of Henry MacLeod, to reach the icefield.

POSSIBLE EXTENSIONS: Valad Peak is most reasonably combined with nearby Mount Henry MacLeod by following scree slopes to the summit from the MacLeod/Valad col. It is also possible, though not recommended, to continue northwards to the Valad/Brazeau col on a mix of loose rock and heavily crevassed glacier to reach the start of the ascent slope for Mount Brazeau (see p204).

Descending Mount Henry MacLeod to reach the MacLeod/Valad col.
Photo: Steven Song.

Looking north from near the summit of Mount Henry MacLeod, showing the route to Valad Peak (V). Photo: Steven Song.

Difficulty:
mountaineering (glacier travel; steep snow; 4th, PD–)

Hazards:
rockfall; crevasses; avalanches

Round-trip distance:
16 km
(from high camp below Valad Peak)

Total elevation gain:
1400 m
(from high camp below Valad Peak)

Round-trip time:
8–13 hours
(from high camp below Valad Peak)

Recommended seasons:
summer; fall

Maps:
83C06 Sunwapta Peak;
83C11 Southesk Lake

*William Warren was a guide and packer for Mary Schäffer's expeditions in the early 1900s. Mount Warren has only recently gained acceptance in the exclusive club of Canadian Rockies 11,000ers and is sure to see more traffic in future years by peakbaggers chasing the list.*

ACCESS: Via Hwy 93, 72 km south of Jasper or 81 km north of Saskatchewan Crossing. Park on the east side of the highway, on the south side of Poboktan Creek. The trail starts on the north side of the creek, beside the warden station (walk across the bridge from the parking area to access it).

APPROACH: Follow the approach to the Brazeau Icefield bivy site as described on p203. Allow 6–8 hours to reach the site from the highway. While Mount Warren is possible as a day trip from the bivy site, many parties will want to make a high-camp

As seen from the glacier below Mount Brazeau, the route crosses two sections of flat glacier, a scree ramp and a snow slope before reaching the corniced summit ridge.

Sticking near the rock band on skier's right minimizes the risk of crevasses while making your way to the lower icefield.

somewhere on the icefield to enable a more relaxed pace. A good place to bivy is on the flat section of the icefield below Valad Peak (near GR 770208). Be sure to probe vigilantly for crevasses, especially later in the climbing season. Allow 3–4 hours to reach the high camp from the regular Brazeau Icefield bivy site (18 km and 1700 m of elevation gain from the road).

Leave the Brazeau Icefield bivy site and follow the ascent route for Mount Brazeau described on p204 as it winds up the Brazeau Icefield toward the glaciated slopes below Valad Peak near GR 770208. A direct line down the icefield to the lower glacier via the bowl below Mount Brazeau is not recommended, due to extensive crevasses. Instead aim for the rocky outcrop to the northeast and descend 100 vertical metres on scree-covered ice near GR 773212. Take great care not to descend the slope too far to the west, which is home to mammoth crevasses. Once on the lower icefield, work your way to the northeast, staying on the mellow terrain near the unnamed rock ridge above. Stay wary of crevasses the entire way when traversing the icefield; later in the summer, progress can be difficult due to the extensive route-finding this crevasse avoidance will entail. Near the end of the rock ridge, a gentle glacial slope near GR 781227 leads down onto the flats. From here, angle westwards, making a beeline for the prominent scree/snow band below the south slopes of Mount Warren. Ascend the loose scree for 200 vertical metres to reach the upper Warren glacier. Once on the upper glacier, make your way to the east ridge of Mount Warren by negotiating a path through the bergschrund. In the earlier season, expect decent snow on this nearly 40 degree slope for the remaining 400 m to the summit ridge. In drier years, or later in the season, this section can involve several pitches of ice with considerable exposure above the southeast face of the peak. Once on the summit ridge, carry on over undulating glacial terrain as you work your way towards the summit. Partway along the ridge, the true high point is reached, though maps credit the more westerly high point visible from the lake as the official summit. Take care on the summit ridge to avoid both the large cornice on the northern side and several crevasses that lurk along the slope. The view of Maligne Lake from the summit is almost too good to be true. Take care on descent and remain vigilant in probing for crevasses.

## "BIVY RIDGE" (GR 780175), 2766 M

**Difficulty:**
easy scramble (3rd, F)

**Hazards:**
rockfall; early-season avalanches

**Round-trip distance:**
30 km

**Total elevation gain:**
1400 m

**Round-trip time:**
2 days

**Recommended seasons:**
summer; fall

**Maps:**
83C06 Sunwapta Peak;
83C11 Southesk Lake

*"Bivy Ridge" is an unofficial name for a minor ridge near the normal Brazeau Icefield bivy site. For mountaineers, this is a good way to burn a little extra energy after setting up camp. For less technical peakbaggers, the ridge offers good views and none of the complications associated with glacier travel.*

ACCESS: Via Hwy 93, 72 km south of Jasper or 81 km north of Saskatchewan Crossing. Park on the east side of the highway, on the south side of Poboktan Creek. The trail starts on the north side of the creek, beside the warden station (walk across the bridge from the parking area to access it).

The summit of the ridge provides excellent views of the lower Brazeau Icefield and many unnamed peaks to the east. The approximate line to gain the icefield from the bivy site (B) is shown.

A sunset view southward from the Brazeau Icefield bivy site towards "Bivy Ridge" (B). The route passes the col (C) used on the way up from the valley before ascending a short gully to gain the ridge.

APPROACH: Via Poboktan Creek Trail and then the Brazeau Icefield approach. See the entry for Mount Brazeau at p203 for details. Allow 6–8 hours to reach the bivy site from the highway. The route begins at the Brazeau Icefield bivy site.

From the bivy site, head south towards the col between the ascent gully and "Bivy Ridge." Ascend rubbly scree to a prominent notch that affords passage to the upper ridge (be careful of rockfall in this notch). Once on the ridge, ascend easy scree to the cairned summit. If time and energy allow, traversing the ridge down to the southeast has good views and a small meltwater pond. Allow an hour round-trip from the bivy site.

Difficulty:
easy scramble (2nd, F)

Hazards:
rockfall; early-season
avalanches

Round-trip distance:
38 km

Total elevation gain:
2100 m

Round-trip time:
2–3 days

Recommended seasons:
summer; fall

Map:
83C06 Sunwapta Peak

*"Poboktan" is a Stoney Nakoda word for "owl." And Poboktan Mountain is sure to be a hoot for those peakbaggers eager for a straightforward way to a high summit. While possible as a day trip, the authors recommend spending the night at one of the campgrounds along the Poboktan Creek trail.*

ACCESS: Via Hwy 93, 72 km south of Jasper or 81 km north of Saskatchewan Crossing. Park on the east side of the highway, on the south side of Poboktan Creek. The trail starts on the north side of the creek, beside the warden station (walk across the bridge from the parking area to access it).

Straightforward hiking terrain to ascend Poboktan Mountain. Photo: Vern Dewit.

The ascent line for Poboktan as seen from nearby Sunwapta Peak.
Photo: Eric Coulthard.

APPROACH: From the warden station, set off on the Poboktan Creek trail, which is well maintained and quite popular with peakbaggers and hikers alike. There are two hiker campgrounds near the peak: Poboktan at 7.4 km from the road; and Waterfalls, a further 4.5 km along the trail. The authors recommend staying at Waterfalls Campground if possible (in the peak of the summer be sure to reserve early). Allow 4–5 hours from the highway to reach the campground.

From Waterfalls Campground, carry on southeast along the trail for a little under 4 km before branching off into the bush on the climber's left (northeast) side of the trail. The forest is very thin here and bushwhacking is surprisingly pleasant by Jasper standards. Make a rising traverse up 250 vertical metres to reach treeline. Here marks the start of the lengthy scree slope leading to the summit. From treeline there is still 1100 metres of elevation to gain, but progress gives increasingly impressive views when you look behind you. Carry on up scree slopes to the summit ridge. The true summit lies on the eastern edge of the ridge, and on a warm day it is a fantastic viewpoint for a well-deserved lunch. Follow the same line on the way down.

Difficulty:
easy scramble (2nd, F)

Hazards:
rockfall; early-season
avalanches

Round-trip distance:
26 km

Total elevation gain:
1200 m

Round-trip time:
10–12 hours

Recommended seasons:
summer; fall

Maps:
83C06 Sunwapta Peak;
83C11 Southesk Lake

*Named in 1923 by Howard Palmer, Replica from certain angles was thought to closely match the profile of nearby Mount Brazeau (albeit a much lower version).*

ACCESS: Via Hwy 93, 72 km south of Jasper or 81 km north of Saskatchewan Crossing. Park on the east side of the highway, on the south side of Poboktan Creek. The trail starts on the north side of the creek, beside the warden station (walk across the bridge from the parking area to access it).

APPROACH: From the warden station, head eastwards on Poboktan Creek Trail. At 6 km you'll reach a junction with the

Replica Peak is a long ridge separating the Poligne Valley from Coronet Creek and Coronet Mountain (where this photo was taken). Photo: Steven Song.

LE GRAND BRAZEAU REPLICA PEAK

The Endless Chain Ridge seen from the summit is somewhat less fearsome on its eastern slopes compared to the slabs on the western face seen from the Icefields Parkway.

unsigned Maligne Pass trail on your left. Though officially decommissioned, this trail is still in good shape and allows for quick travel up the Poligne Valley. After 2 km the trail winds westwards, leading up to the meadows and lakes around Maligne Pass. Just over 11 km from the trailhead you'll reach Avalanche Campground. If you are breaking your ascent into two days, this is a preferred place to camp. As of 2014, Parks began enforcing a quota for the Maligne Pass area, allowing only one party at a time to obtain an overnight camping permit. Check at the visitor centre in Jasper as to the current policy before setting off.

From Avalanche Campground, continue heading northwest towards Maligne Pass while the long ridge of Replica Peak rises up to your right. Once you leave the bush at around GR 701169, start ascending the peak via loose, steep scree. This scree slope leads upwards at a fairly comfortable grade until around 2700 metres, where a final, steeper scree slope must be ascended to break through the summit slabs (look for the slope just to climber's left of a shallow rock gully). Once above this steep patch, you reach the summit. Views down towards Maligne Pass are spectacular, as is the panorama of nearby peaks of the Brazeau Icefield and more distant giants to the south on the Columbia Icefield. On the way down, angling skier's right and spending a few hours hiking around Maligne Pass is highly recommended. Once you have had your fill of the sublime alpine sights, regain the trail anywhere below the peak and follow it back to the highway.

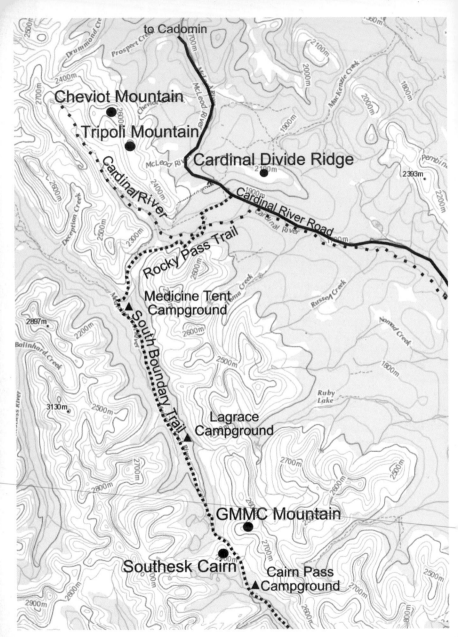

to Cadomin

Cheviot Mountain

Tripoli Mountain

Cardinal Divide Ridge

Cardinal River

Cardinal River Road

Rocky Pass Trail

Medicine Tent
Campground

South Boundary Trail

Lagrace
Campground

GMMC Mountain

Southesk Cairn

Cairn Pass
Campground

Ruby
Lake

# SOUTH BOUNDARY TRAIL AND WHITEHORSE WILDLAND PROVINCIAL PARK

| MOUNTAIN | ELEVATION (M) | ROUTE TYPE | PAGE |
|---|---|---|---|
| **South Boundary Trail** | | | |
| • Southesk Cairn | 2575 | Moderate scramble | 222 |
| • GMMC Mountain | 2825 | Moderate scramble | 224 |
| **Whitehorse Wildland Provincial Park** | | | |
| • Cardinal Divide Ridge | 2220 | On-trail hike | 226 |
| • Tripoli Mountain | 2625 | Difficult scramble | 228 |
| • Cheviot Mountain | 2730 | Easy scramble | 230 |

## AREA OVERVIEW

South Boundary Trail, one of the longest backcountry routes in the Canadian Rockies, parallels the south (and east) boundary of Jasper National Park. Originally, the trail extended from Nigel Pass along the Icefields Parkway in the south to Medicine Lake along Maligne Lake Road (a distance of over 160 km). The modern South Boundary Trail is less lengthy, owing to forest fires in 2003 and 2006 which created significant deadfall along the northern reaches of the trail. As a result of these complications, and the loss of several bridges, Parks officially decommissioned the northern section of the trail. However, as with many other decommissioned trails, the route is still very much traversable if you can tolerate sustained bushwhacking and unbridged stream crossings. The remaining portion of the original trail, from Nigel Pass to Rocky Pass, affords access to some very remote terrain with boundless options for peakbagging. This chapter describes the section of trail from Rocky Pass to Cairn Pass. Be prepared for long approaches but splendid isolation when peakbagging in this area. For a complete description of the route see Brian Patton and Bart Robinson's *The Canadian Rockies Trail Guide*.

Sharing a parking area with the South Boundary trail is the Cardinal River Headwaters trail, part of Whitehorse Wildland Provincial Park. This 175 km$^2$ park, established in 1998, is home to numerous peaks and critters, and oddly enough it borders an active coal mine. For more information about Whitehorse Wildland, visit albertaparks.ca/whitehorse.aspx.

## ACCESS, ACCOMMODATIONS AND FACILITIES

To reach the trailhead from Jasper, drive 72 km northeast on Hwy 16 to

its junction with Hwy 40 just before Hinton. At the junction, turn south and follow Hwy 40 for 52 km to the hamlet of Cadomin. From Cadomin head south via the Cardinal River road, which passes through the Cheviot Creek mining site and then leads to the signed Cardinal River Headwaters parking lot (22 km from Cadomin). **Note** that on some maps Cardinal River Road is labelled Gravel Flats Road.

A scenic series of waterfalls called "The Punchbowls" can be seen on the way to South Boundary Trail.
Photo: Eric Coulthard.

There are no backcountry lodges, tea houses or other commercial developments on the South Boundary Trail or in Whitehorse Wildland Park, but some limited supplies can be obtained from the general store in Cadomin (be warned that this store also has very limited business hours). A considerably wider selection of supplies is available in Hinton, on Hwy 16 a few kilometres past the Hwy 40 junction.

There are three hiker campsites along the South Boundary trail

Open meadows at Rocky Pass on the boundary of Jasper National Park.
Photo: Eric Coulthard.

between Rocky Pass and Cairn Pass which can be reserved by contacting the Jasper National Park visitor centre. Random camping is permitted in Whitehorse Wildland Provincial Park except at Cardinal Divide (as of 2016 no reservations were required and no fee was charged).

## PERMITS AND RESTRICTIONS

The described routes along the South Boundary trail lie within Jasper National Park and thus are subject to restrictions. Obtain more information from Parks Canada in Jasper or their website. Backcountry camping is restricted to specific areas; contact Parks for details.

Peaks in Whitehorse Wildland Provincial Park are subject to similar restrictions as are found in the national parks in terms of hunting, fishing and open fires. The provincial park further prohibits biking except on designated trails. Contact Alberta Parks or visit their website for current information on policies.

The unprotected areas bordering this region are prime terrain for recreational hunters during the fall months. Wearing bright clothing and making a lot of noise while heading through the bush during this time of year is recommended to avoid possible encounters with hunters.

## SOUTHESK CAIRN, 2575 M ☐

Difficulty:
moderate scramble (3rd, F)

Hazards:
rockfall; early-season
avalanches

Round-trip distance:
51 km

Total elevation gain:
1700 m

Round-trip time:
3–4 days

Recommended seasons:
summer; fall

Maps:
83C11 Southesk Lake;
83C14 Mountain Park

*Named in 1859, Southesk Cairn commemorates the journey of James Carnegie, the Earl of Southesk, who famously styled himself the first tourist in the region. Legend has it that the cairn atop the peak was first built by his hand. In 2009 the modern-day Earl of Southesk, James George Alexander Bannerman Carnegie, and his family visited the site and reassembled the cairn to celebrate the 150th anniversary of the event.*

ACCESS: Via the Cardinal River road. The access route for South Boundary Trail starts from the Cardinal River Headwaters parking lot, 22 km south of Cadomin.

The Southesk Cairn ascent route starts on the northeastern slopes before traversing onto the north face. Photo: Eric Coulthard.

The scramble to the false summit of Southesk Cairn (SC) is straightforward but loose in places. Photo: Eric Coulthard.

APPROACH: From parking, set out on the broad seismic line that points southwest. Follow this for a little over 2 km until you reach an open meadow. While the seismic line carries on due southwest, the trail leads to climber's left (southeast), crossing the Cardinal River. Keep following this trail, eventually reaching the Jasper Park boundary at Rocky Pass (around GR 806555). The route then descends towards the valley through a series of steep switchbacks before eventually reaching the Medicine Tent campground, some 11 km from the trailhead. From here there are two options for campsites: traveling south a further 10 km to Lagrace campground or 15 km to Cairn Pass campground. The authors recommend the latter option, which though 2 km past Southesk Cairn, rewards peakbaggers with good views and (likely) solitude.

From the Cairn Pass campground, head back towards Cairn Pass, aiming for the southwest face of Southesk Cairn around GR 907403. Ascend scree slopes while traversing to climber's right onto the north face of the peak, breaking through a small patch of cliffbands with moderate scrambling. Carry on around the peak until you reach the northwest ridge, which is then followed to the summit. On descent, either retrace your steps or follow scree ramps on the west face down to Cairn Lakes. From the lakes, return to camp and then follow the same route back to the road. **Note** that on some maps Cairn Pass is called Southesk Pass.

POSSIBLE EXTENSION: Southesk Cairn can be readily combined with GMMC Mountain to the north of Cairn Pass (see p224 for details).

Difficulty:
moderate scramble (3rd, F)

Hazards:
rockfall; early-season
avalanches

Round-trip distance:
53 km

Total elevation gain:
1950 m

Round-trip time:
3–4 days

Recommended seasons:
summer; fall

Maps:
83C11 Southesk Lake;
83C14 Mountain Park

*This peak across the valley from Southesk Cairn was first ascended in 2007 by Edmonton's Grant MacEwan Mountain Club. Hence its unofficial name based on the club's initials.*

ACCESS: Via the Cardinal River road. The access route for South Boundary Trail starts from the Cardinal River Headwaters parking lot, 22 km south of Cadomin.

APPROACH: Via Rocky Pass Trail and South Boundary Trail. See Southesk Cairn on p222 for details. The route for GMMC Mountain starts from Cairn Pass Campground.

The route up the south slopes of GMMC Mountain as seen from Southesk Cairn. The location of the crux traverse (C) is shown. Photo: Eric Coulthard.

A bit of interesting scrambling to be done at the crux section of GMMC Mountain.
Photo: Eric Coulthard.

There is plenty of idyllic scenery to check out while in the area.
Photo: Eric Coulthard.

From the campground, head north, back towards Cairn Pass. The ascent slope for GMMC Mountain is readily visible from the pass, and the route starts from the base of the gully between GMMC and the lower, unnamed summit to the southwest. Ascend the slope for 400 vertical metres before reaching the crux, a steep traverse of moderate scrambling terrain shown below. Past the crux, continue upwards on the ridgecrest to reach the summit. Follow the same route back to the campground on descent.

POSSIBLE EXTENSION: While in the area an ascent of Southesk Cairn is highly recommended (see p222).

Difficulty:
on-trail hike (2nd, F)

Hazards:
few

Round-trip distance:
8 km

Total elevation gain:
250 m

Round-trip time:
2–3 hours

Recommended seasons:
spring; summer; fall

Map:
83C14 Mountain Park

*This decent viewpoint takes its unofficial name from the Cardinal River. The river itself was named for Jacques Cardinal, an employee of the Hudson's Bay Company who served as a guide for the Earl of Southesk on his famous journey to Southesk Cairn.*

ACCESS: Via the Cardinal River road. The signed trailhead is at the Cardinal Divide viewpoint some 20 km south of Cadomin.

APPROACH: Directly from the road; follow the trail.

Follow the trail as it gradually winds up to the long, flat ridge. Enjoy the restful grade and views to the south and west (the view to the north towards the Cheviot Mine is less glamorous). Traverse down the ridge for as long as you like and return the way you came.

The wide ATV trail that leads up to the broad, flat top of the ridge.
Photo: Eric Coulthard.

Cardinal Divide Ridge is a good viewpoint for looking west towards Jasper National Park. Photo: Eric Coulthard.

**Difficulty:**
difficult scramble (4th, F)

**Hazards:**
rockfall

**Round-trip distance:**
14 km

**Total elevation gain:**
800 m

**Round-trip time:**
6–8 hours

**Recommended seasons:**
summer; fall

**Map:**
83C14 Mountain Park

*This peak was named in 1922 for reasons unknown. Tripoli is the current capital of Libya as well as the name of a city in northern Lebanon and several settlements in ancient Greece. For peakbaggers, Tripoli Mountain offers good scrambling and a variety of views.*

ACCESS: Via the Cardinal River road. The signed trailhead is at the Cardinal Divide viewpoint, 20 km south of Cadomin.

APPROACH: From the parking area head southwest along a broad trail as it heads towards the ridge south of Tripoli Mountain.

After following the trail for 2 km, head west near the base of the ridge and aim to ascend the broad gully near GR 794595. A gradually rising traverse sorts out the 300 vertical metres between the valley and ridge-crest. Once on the ridge, carry on north-west towards the summit, passing by two unnamed summits before reaching the base of the south ridge of Tripoli Mountain. Stick near the crest while ascending the ridge on moderate to difficult scrambling terrain. A steep, exposed rock step halfway up the ridge gives a particular challenge for would-be summiteers. Retrace your steps on descent.

Below opposite page: The crux of the south ridge of Tripoli Mountain is the short but very exposed step shown here on descent. The ascent and descent lines carry on down the southeast ridge before reaching gentler terrain on the east face (out of view). Photo: Eric Coulthard.

The ascent ridge for Tripoli Mountain (T) contains a variety of difficult and moderate scrambling with one exposed section (shown as E). In the background is Cheviot Mountain (C). Photo: Eric Coulthard.

Difficulty:
easy scramble (2nd, F)

Hazards:
rockfall

Round-trip distance:
21 km

Total elevation gain:
1100 m

Round-trip time:
8–10 hours

Recommended seasons:
summer; fall

Map:
83C14 Mountain Park

*This peak is named for a group of well-known hills along the English–Scottish border. An early traveller to the Rockies thought Cheviot Mountain resembled The Cheviot, the highest peak in that range, which boasts an "impressive" elevation of 815 m. Just for comparison, the Cardinal Divide viewpoint sits at an elevation of 1850 m.*

ACCESS: Via the Cardinal River road. The signed trailhead is at the Cardinal Divide viewpoint, 20 km south of Cadomin.

APPROACH: The most efficient route up Cheviot Mountain ascends the unnamed ridge south of Tripoli Mountain.

Steven Song saunters up the slopes of Cheviot Mountain (C), taking the scenic route to first gain the summit ridge. Photo: Eric Coulthard.

C

After you've traversed the south ridge of Tripoli Mountain, the latter portion of the route drops down into the valley and ascends Cheviot's southwest ridge.
Photo: Eric Coulthard.

Follow the route for Tripoli Mountain (p228) until reaching the base of the south-facing ascent ridge of Tripoli Mountain. Carry on westward, losing 200 metres of elevation while sidehilling towards the broad bowl south of Cheviot Mountain. Ascend scree to reach the col between Cheviot and a lower, unnamed peak before gaining the southwest ridge, which is then followed to the summit. Return the way you came.

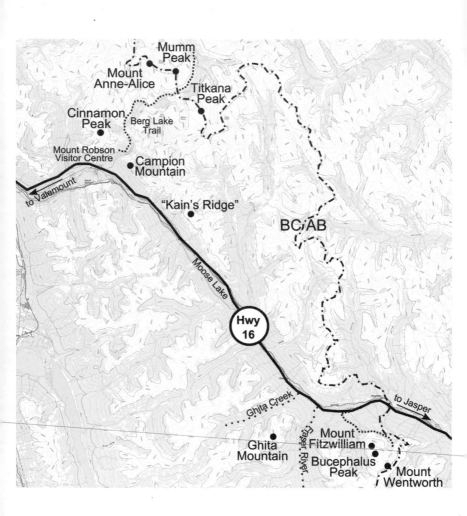

Mumm Peak

Mount Anne-Alice

Titkana Peak

Cinnamon Peak

Berg Lake Trail

Mount Robson Visitor Centre

Campion Mountain

to Valemount

"Kain's Ridge"

BC AB

Moose Lake

Hwy 16

Ghita Creek

to Jasper

Fraser River

Ghita Mountain

Mount Fitzwilliam

Bucephalus Peak

Mount Wentworth

# MOUNT ROBSON PROVINCIAL PARK

| MOUNTAIN | ELEVATION (M) | ROUTE TYPE | PAGE |
|----------|---------------|------------|------|
| Cinnamon Peak | 2723 | Difficult scramble | 238 |
| Campion Mountain | 2135 | Easy scramble | 242 |
| Titkana Peak * | 2804 | Easy scramble | 244 |
| Mumm Peak | 2963 | Alpine climb (5.3) | 246 |
| Mount Anne-Alice | 3023 | Mountaineering | 250 |
| Mount Fitzwilliam | 2902 | Moderate scramble | 252 |
| Bucephalus Peak | 2763 | Moderate scramble | 254 |
| Mount Wentworth | 2715 | Moderate scramble | 256 |
| Ghita Mountain | 2531 | Easy scramble | 258 |
| "Kain's Ridge" (GR 648769) | 2300 | Easy scramble | 260 |

## AREA OVERVIEW

Beyond the western boundary of Jasper National Park lies one of the gems of the Rockies, Mount Robson Provincial Park, home to the highest peak in the range along with many enjoyable routes and lovely lakes. While not large compared to nearby Jasper National Park (only 2253 square kilometres), Mount Robson Provincial Park is certainly a must-see destination for all peakbaggers.

## ACCESS, ACCOMMODATIONS AND FACILITIES

There is only one road through Mount Robson Provincial Park: Hwy 16, the Yellowhead. Hwy 16 can be accessed from either Jasper to the east (from Hinton via Hwy 16 or Saskatchewan Crossing via Hwy 93), McBride to the west (via Hwy 16) or Valemount to the southwest (via Hwy 5).

There are numerous campsites, both roadside and backcountry, in the park. Camping permits can be obtained from BC Parks' "Discover Camping" website at secure.camis.com/Discovercamping or at the visitor centre. Reservations are first come first served, and sites along the Berg Lake trail can book up months ahead of time in the popular summer season. As of 2016 no fees were charged, nor permits required, for winter camping in the park.

Food and supplies can be obtained in Valemount, with a wider selection possible by carrying on eastward to Jasper. During the summer months, gas and snacks are available, at a premium, beside the Mount Robson visitor centre.

Mount Robson itself is without a doubt the star attraction of this region. Berg Lake Trail, from Kinney Lake to Berg Lake, can be seen from the summit of Cinnamon Peak as shown here.

## PERMITS AND RESTRICTIONS

Frontcountry camping in the park (and backcountry camping along Berg Lake Trail) is restricted to designated regions and requires permits, which can be obtained at the Mount Robson visitor centre just off Hwy 16, in the shadow of Mount Robson itself. Talk to staff at the centre for current policies on random backcountry camping.

Up-to-date information about practices and policies in the park can be obtained at the official Robson webpage, www.env.gov.bc.ca/bcparks/explore/parkpgs/mt_robson.

## BERG LAKE TRAIL

Berg Lake Trail is without a doubt the most popular route in Mount Robson Provincial Park. The track is very well maintained and very well travelled. For peakbaggers the route allows for straightforward access to the peaks surrounding Berg Lake and provides numerous options for camping. There are seven official campgrounds along the trail, all of which require overnight permits. During the peak summer season, campsites can be quite difficult to secure, but normally by September things have wound down and peakbaggers can more easily decide to camp up the trail on a whim. The first 7 km of the trail, to the Kinney Lake campground, can be biked to speed up the approach. Take note that bikes are not allowed on the rest of the trail. The largest campground, at Berg Lake itself, is 21 km from the trailhead with 800 metres of elevation gain and is the recommended starting point for several of the routes described in this section. All overnight users of the trail must attend a short orientation session at the visitor centre before starting their trip. Take note that the area around Snowbird Pass is closed during May and June to protect calving caribou.

Check the park's webpage and with Parks staff at the visitor centre for trail conditions and current policies.

There is plenty of remote terrain to be explored in Mount Robson Provincial Park, including the valley below Mount Kain shown here.

## CINNAMON PEAK, 2723 M ☐

Difficulty:
difficult scramble (4th, F)

Hazards:
rockfall; early-season
avalanches

Round-trip distance:
12 km

Total elevation gain:
2300 m

Round-trip time:
12–15 hours·

Recommended seasons:
summer; fall

Map:
83E03 Mount Robson

*Named for the resemblance between the colour of rock on the peak and the fur of a grizzly bear, Cinnamon Peak is one of the best viewpoints in the park. Expect excellent views of Mount Robson and Whitehorn Mountain as well as the sea of peaks along the North Boundary Trail.*

ACCESS: From the Berg Lake trailhead, accessed via Kinney Lake Road. Drive 37 km north and east from Valemount or 87 km west from Jasper on Hwy 16 to the Mount Robson visitor centre. Turn north onto Kinney Lake Road and follow it to the trailhead.

APPROACH: From the Berg Lake trailhead, follow the trail for a little over 800 m until you arrive beneath a large bushy slope to your left. Before setting off up this slope, gather your wits and prepare for some suffocating alder-bashing.

Once your nose is firmly in the bush, head upwards aiming for the middle of the drainage. After 200 vertical metres the bush lets up and the terrain transitions to boulders. At this point you still have 800 vertical metres to gain in this gully over a mix of short rock bands, grassy ledges and creek crossings. The water-worn rock in the gully is exceptionally smooth and very slippery even when dry. Try to stay on the

Ascending Cinnamon Peak requires a long climb in the prominent gully before traversing to gain the east ridge leading to the summit. Photo: Steven Song.

climber's right side of the creek when possible. Eventually the gully broadens and the east ridge becomes visible. To gain the ridge, enter a broad bowl about 400 metres above the gully on climber's right. Gain the east ridge by traversing back and forth on ledges above the bowl. Continue heading upwards on the crest of the ridge for 300 vertical metres until you reach a prominent false summit complete with a weather tower. The true summit is on the other side of a high col which requires descending the northwest ridge (losing approximately 100 metres) along moderate scrambling terrain with a few difficult moves. Ascending to the true summit requires difficult scrambling on loose rock; stay close together to minimize rockfall hazard. At long last the summit cairn is reached. Be careful not to spend too much time on the summit, as it is still a long way back down to the road. Retrace your steps back down. Resist the temptation to follow the rock path down to avoid alders, as this will only lead to prickly patches of devil's club.

Above the gully the terrain opens up considerably

Difficulty:
easy scramble (3rd, F)

Hazards:
few

Round-trip distance:
8 km

Total elevation gain:
1200 m

Round-trip time:
7–9 hours

Recommended season:
winter (snowshoes)

ATES rating:
challenging

Map:
83E03 Mount Robson

*Silene acaulis, or moss campion, is a pink alpine wildflower found in many ranges of North America and Europe. The upper slopes of Campion Mountain are decorated with many of these visually pleasing plants. The challenges of ascending Campion are purely mental: maintaining focus while climbing through 1000 metres of bush. But the summit views make the slog well worthwhile. A good supportive snowpack and a sturdy set of snowshoes let a peakbagger rise above the lower foliage and as such a winter ascent is recommended.*

ACCESS: Via Hwy 16. Park on the side of the highway 4.5 km east of the Mount Robson visitor centre (41.5 km east of Valemount or 82.5 km west of Jasper).

APPROACH: Set off up the peak right from the side of the highway.

From the roadside pick a line directly up the mountain. The majority of the mountain consists of moderately dense bush and moderately steep slopes. Don't become discouraged, though: after 2 km distance and 800 metres of elevation gain, the trees start to thin and you will emerge with views of an alpine paradise and one of the best viewpoints of Mount Robson around. Once on the summit ridge, at an elevation of 2000 metres, head westwards up to the summit. If you have extra energy the ridge leading eastwards to an unnamed peak can be explored for a while before the terrain becomes more technical. After you have finished admiring the scenery, retrace your steps back down to the road.

Many ascent lines are possible on the broad, bushy south face of Campion Mountain (C) as seen from Cinnamon Peak. Photo: Steven Song.

Looking back towards Moose Lake from treeline on Campion Mountain. Photo: Steven Song.

Difficulty:
easy scramble (2nd, F)

Hazards:
rockfall; early-season avalanches

Round-trip distance:
21 km
(from Berg Lake Campground)

Total elevation gain:
1650 m
(from Berg Lake Campground)

Round-trip time:
9–11 hours

Recommended seasons:
summer; fall

Map:
83E03 Mount Robson

*"Titkana" is a Stoney Nakoda word for "bird," and the peak certainly grants the peak-bagger a bird's-eye view of Robson Glacier and nearby peaks. Titkana Peak is the high point on the western edge of Tatei Ridge. The route described here traverses Tatei Ridge and is an exceptionally scenic line, with views of the Reef Icefield as well as Mount Robson and countless other peaks.*

ACCESS: From the Berg Lake trailhead, accessed via Kinney Lake Road. Drive 37 km east of Valemount or 87 km west of Jasper on Hwy 16 to the Mount Robson visitor centre. Turn north onto Kinney Lake Road and follow it to the trailhead.

APPROACH: Via Berg Lake Trail (see p235). The route starts from the Berg Lake campground, 21 km from the trailhead.

The route up Titkana Peak (T) follows Snowbird Pass Trail and then winds up the scree slopes leading to the summit ridge. In the distance is Lynx Mountain (L). Photo: Vern Dewit.

Views from the summit ridge are awe-inspiring. Photo: Vern Dewit.

From Berg Lake Campground, head northeast towards Hargreaves Shelter and follow the signed Snowbird Pass Trail as it traverses on the edge of Robson Glacier. Once you have passed the creek descending from Snowbird Meadows, the trail winds upward towards the gap between Titkana Peak and Lynx Mountain. After reaching the meadows, leave the trail trending west (climber's left) and aim for the long scree ridge leading to the ridge. While ascending the easy terrain to reach the ridge be sure to stop to admire the views behind you! After you top out on the ridge, easy scree leads all the way to the true summit. On descent, either return the way you came or go down the ridge directly below the summit. Either way will lead you back to Snowbird Meadows, from where you can then return down Snowbird Pass Trail.

Difficulty:
alpine climb (5.3, PD−)

Hazards:
rockfall; early-season
avalanches

Round-trip distance:
12 km
(from Berg Lake
Campground)

Total elevation gain:
1200 m
(from Berg Lake
Campground)

Round-trip time:
8–10 hours
(from Berg Lake
Campground)

Recommended seasons:
summer; fall

Map:
83E03 Mount Robson

*Named for Arnold L. Mumm, a well-known early explorer in the Canadian Rockies and a lifetime member of the Alpine Club of Canada.*

ACCESS: From the Berg Lake trailhead, accessed via Kinney Lake Road. Drive 37 km east of Valemount or 87 km west of Jasper on Hwy 16 to the Mount Robson visitor centre. Turn north onto Kinney Lake Road and follow it to the trailhead.

APPROACH: Via Berg Lake Trail (see p235). The route starts from the Berg Lake campground, 21 km from the trailhead.

From the campground, follow the Robson Pass trail towards the Robson Pass campground 2 km from the Berg Lake campground. At the Robson Pass junction, head north up Mumm Basin Trail for 2 km until you reach an excellent viewpoint with a large cairn. From the cairn leave the trail and head upwards, parallel with the Alberta boundary, heading up scree slopes to a false summit which is itself an outstanding viewpoint. Carry on upwards past the false summit, aiming for the intimidating summit block that rises 700 metres above. Before you reach the summit block there is a permanent snow patch lingering from an old extinct glacier. Rangers in the area confirm that the snowpatch is free of crevasses but parties could don a rope for peace of mind (a rope is advised for the technical summit block). The ascent chimney is to climber's left of the summit block and is marked with a stuck red sling (see image below). Ascending the chimney requires a few

The chimney you can use to access the summit block seen here in less than ideal conditions.

M

technical moves and belaying the pitch is recommended especially if conditions are wet or icy. The crux move involves climbing over a chockstone. After the crux, work your way carefully higher on extremely exposed terrain to reach the first (west) summit. The traverse to the true (east) summit is quite exposed and some parties may feel much more comfortable with a belay. On descent, rappelling the chimney is advisable. Below the summit block retrace your steps back down the trail to return to the campground.

Opposite: The route up Mumm Peak (M) from near Berg Lake.

Below: Impressive views from near the summit of Mumm Peak. Photo: Vern Dewit

**Difficulty:**
mountaineering (glacier travel; 3rd, F)

**Hazards:**
rockfall; crevasses; avalanches

**Round-trip distance:**
12 km
(from Berg Lake Campground)

**Total elevation gain:**
1450 m
(from Berg Lake Campground)

**Round-trip time:**
8–11 hours
(from Berg Lake Campground)

**Recommended seasons:**
summer; fall; winter (skis)

**Map:**
83E03 Mount Robson

*Named for Anne Chesser and Alice Wright, who first ascended the peak in 1939, Mount Anne-Alice (a naming trend which works best for two-person groups) is an outstanding viewpoint and a worthwhile day trip from Berg Lake.*

ACCESS: From the Berg Lake trailhead, accessed via Kinney Lake Road. Drive 37 km east of Valemount or 87 km west of Jasper on Hwy 16 to the Mount Robson visitor centre. Turn north onto Kinney Lake Road and follow it to the trailhead.

APPROACH: Via Berg Lake Trail (see p235). The route starts from the Berg Lake campground, 21 km from the trailhead.

From the campground, follow the trail to Hargreaves Shelter and carry on northeast to the signed start of Toboggan Falls Trail. Carry on upwards as the trail winds beside Toboggan Creek, reaches the falls

From upper Toboggan Creek the route ascends a steep slope to reach the Steamboat/Anne-Alice col (C) and then follows the wide ridge upwards to the false summit (F).

Views from the false summit are very impressive, especially the broken glacier of Mount Philips (P). The true summit (A) is reached by descending briefly onto the glacier before gaining the ridge.

themselves and then continues upwards into the basin above. After 300 vertical metres from the campground you will reach treeline and enter into a broad network of rocky gentle ribs. Take a good look at the ascent col (see the Steamboat/Anne-Alice col photo on p250) and work your way upwards towards the base of the slope. In dry conditions reaching the col can be a steep scramble on loose scree; stick close together to minimize rockfall hazard. Once atop the col, your work is still far from over, as 500 vertical metres of scrambling on gentle scree stands between you and the false summit. Thankfully, the impressive views of Mount Robson behind and Whitehorn Mountain to the left should keep you motivated! The view from the false summit is stunning, but the true summit beckons you onwards to the northwest. While the route to the false summit is a scramble, a short glacier crossing is required to reach the true summit. Rope up and descend a short snow/ice slope (around 30 degrees) before traversing the bowl and then kicking steps upwards to the summit. Views of Mount Philips, Whitehorn Mountain, Mount Bess and of course Mount Robson, to name only a few, make this one of the premier viewpoints in the Rockies.

## MOUNT FITZWILLIAM, 2902 M        □

Difficulty:
moderate scramble (3rd, F)

Hazards:
rockfall; early-season
avalanches

Round-trip distance:
24 km

Total elevation gain:
2050 m

Round-trip time:
10–12 hours

Recommended seasons:
summer; fall

Map:
83D15 Lucerne

*One of the most impressive peaks along the Yellowhead Highway in Mount Robson Provincial Park, Mount Fitzwilliam can be climbed as a lengthy (but enjoyable) day trip from the highway or a more comfortable overnight trip camping at Rockingham Creek. The backside (west face) of the peak described here allows for a non-technical ascent line.*

ACCESS: Via Hwy 16. The trailhead is across the highway from the Yellowhead Lake boat launch, 7.3 km west of the Jasper Park boundary. The trail follows the pipeline cutblock for the first 1 km.

Mount Fitzwilliam (F) and Bucephalus Peak (B) as seen from the summit of Ghita Mountain, with their ascent gully and col (C). Photo: Eric Coulthard.

Looking down the ascent gully towards Rockingham Creek. Photo: Steven Song.

APPROACH: Follow the trail up to Fitzwilliam Basin for 7 km until you reach the campsite at Rockingham Creek.

Cross Rockingham Creek using the bridge and then head south along the flats east of the creek. Expect to encounter some bushy patches – you *are* in BC after all! Carry on along the creek for a little under 2 km until you are beneath a prominent gully descending from the Fitzwilliam/Bucephalus col. The bush between the creek and the gully can be very dense in places; a fall ascent is recommended so the foliage will be a little less fearsome. Treeline is reached at an elevation of 2050 metres, after which there is still 600 vertical metres to ascend before reaching the col. The ascent gully (at GR 014536) is full of boulders that can be quite slippery when wet, so stick close together to minimize rockfall hazard. From the col between Mount Fitzwilliam and Bucephalus Peak, stay near the crest of the ridge as you work your way upwards, dropping to climber's left or right when required (terrain here should be only 3rd class). After enjoying the views from the summit, work your way back down to the creek. Resist the urge to descend down towards the tarns in Fitzwilliam Basin: there are large cliffs preventing direct access.

POSSIBLE EXTENSION: If you have extra energy and time, ascending Bucephalus Peak from the Fitzwilliam/Bucephalus col is a worthwhile diversion (see p255).

Difficulty:
moderate scramble (3rd, F)

Hazards:
rockfall; early-season avalanches

Round-trip distance:
23 km

Total elevation gain:
1850 m

Round-trip time:
10–12 hours

Recommended seasons:
summer; fall

Map:
83D15 Lucerne

*While less lofty than nearby Mount Fitzwilliam, Bucephalus Peak is a good viewpoint and worth ascending if you are in the area. The original Bucephalus, translating to "ox-head," was the personal horse of Alexander the Great. Dr. Walter Cheadle named his own horse in honour of this famous beast when he and Fitzwilliam rode through the Rockies in 1863, and decided to dedicate a peak to him.*

ACCESS: Via Hwy 16. The trailhead is across the highway from the Yellowhead Lake boat launch, 7.3 km west of the Jasper Park boundary. The trail follows the pipeline cutblock for the first 1 km.

Bucephalus Peak as seen from near the Fitzwilliam/Bucephalus col. The route stays near the ridgecrest, traversing on the north side. Photo: Steven Song.

Roche Noire (right) is particularly striking from the top of Bucephalus Peak
Photo: Steven Song.

APPROACH: Follow the same approach as described for Mount Fitzwilliam on p253.

The ascent route for Bucephalus Peak follows the same line as for Mount Fitzwilliam until it reaches the Fitzwilliam/Bucephalus col (see p253 for details). From the col there is only a prominent false summit between you and the top. Bypass the false summit by dropping slightly onto the north face, traversing on boulders. Regain the ridgecrest after the false summit and follow the ridge right to the top.

POSSIBLE EXTENSION: While you're in the area an ascent of Mount Fitzwilliam is highly recommended. See p253 for details.

Difficulty:
moderate scramble (3rd, F)

Hazards:
rockfall; early-season
avalanches

Round-trip distance:
31 km

Total elevation gain:
1700 m

Round-trip time:
2 days

Recommended seasons:
summer; fall

Map:
83D15 Lucerne

*Named for William Wentworth Fitzwilliam, whose name also graces nearby Mount Fitzwilliam itself. He and Dr. Walter Cheadle were among the first "tourists" to cross the Rockies, later detailing their experiences in their 1865 book* The Northwest Passage by Land. *While this route is possible as a day trip, the authors recommend an overnight camp in Fitzwilliam Basin to appreciate the remoteness and quality of views.*

Access: Via Hwy 16. The trailhead is across the highway from the Yellowhead Lake boat launch, 7.3 km west of the Jasper Park boundary. The trail follows a pipeline cutblock for the first 1 km.

Approach: From the trailhead there is 13 km of distance and 1000 metres of elevation gain between you and the alpine campsite in Fitzwilliam Basin. The trail can be divided into two distinct sections, with the first 7 km being delightfully maintained, easy hiking up to the Rockingham Creek campground. The trail then crosses Rockingham Creek and the going gets tougher, with plenty of tree roots and boulders making for less efficient travel. Don't lose hope, though: good views await from the higher campground! There are no fees for camping in Fitzwilliam Basin but there is a mandatory sign-in system at the trailhead (look for a green box about 1 km into the trail).

From the alpine campground, traverse around the eastern shore of the lake. Once south of the lake, cross two small creeks while aiming for the large scree bowl joining Mount Wentworth to an unnamed peak to the north (see the image below). Ascend the bowl for 250 vertical metres to the col. Once atop the col, stick near the crest of the ridge, ascending moderate boulders all the way to the summit. Take care to avoid the prominent, slippery snow patches that can linger on the north face into high summer. On a clear day the authors would particularly recommend a sunrise summit for the phenomenal light, especially looking southward towards The Ramparts. When you are done snapping pictures, return the way you came.

Looking up towards Mount Wentworth from the high camp in Fitzwilliam Basin. Photo: Eric Coulthard.

Difficulty:
easy scramble (2nd, F)

Hazards:
early-season avalanches

Round-trip distance:
24 km

Total elevation gain:
1600 m

Round-trip time:
2 days

Recommended season:
winter (skis)

ATES rating:
complex

Map:
83D15 Lucerne

*Named for nearby Ghita Creek, Ghita Mountain has the feel of a remote peak while being only a little over 10 km from the highway. Dense BC bush makes this peak more accessible in winter, when a frozen creek allows for more efficient travel.*

ACCESS: Via Hwy 16. At 15 km west of the Jasper Park boundary, park on either side of the road. Ghita Creek (signed) can be accessed directly from the south side of the road.

APPROACH: Via Ghita Creek. Wait until the creek is frozen before you attempt this route.

Follow Ghita Creek as it winds its way upwards to the head of the valley, towards the heart of the Selwyn Range. The lower parts of the creek are quite isolated by dense bush on either side, so stay in the creek as long as possible. After 4.5 km (and 500 metres of elevation gain) the terrain starts to open up and the creek starts to meander.

Excellent summit views make the bushwhacking on the approach well worthwhile.
Photo: Steven Song.

Continue along the creek past large avalanche gullies descending from the upper ridge until you reach the base of the valley that leads up towards the summit of Ghita Mountain (see the area map on p232 where Ghita Creek is shown). The next 3 km of distance (and 600 metres of elevation) is likely the most tedious part of the trip. Work your way upwards in the creek that drains from the upper valley (near GR 851530), staying in the creek as long as possible to avoid bushwhacking. Occasionally diverging onto the climber's right (south) side may be required. At around 1900 metres elevation start to head eastwards, aiming for the summit. If you are breaking the ascent into two days (recommended by the authors) a high camp near treeline on the south side of the upper creek is advisable. The last 200 metres of elevation will likely involve bootpacking up scree to the summit.

The route first heads up Ghita Creek before ascending into the valley south of Ghita Peak (G).

Past treeline, views open up considerably. Be wary of avalanche hazard while working your way towards the summit (out of view above the ridgecrest).

MOUNT ROBSON PROVINCIAL PARK CHiTA MOUNTAN

Difficulty:
easy scramble (3rd, F)

Hazards:
rockfall; early-season
avalanches

Round-trip distance:
11 km

Total elevation gain:
600 m

Round-trip time:
5–7 hours

Recommended seasons:
summer; fall

Maps:
83D14 Valemount; 83E03
Mount Robson

*Unofficially named for its proximity to nearby Mount Kain (and a vague reference to a similar ridge in* Conrad Kain: Letters from a Wandering Mountain Guide*), this ridge is a great viewpoint for many peaks in Mount Robson Provincial Park and a good day trip.*

ACCESS: Via Hwy 16. Park beside the highway some 3 km west of the western shore of Moose Lake. The parking area is just beside a creek that flows down from the valley surrounding Mount Kain.

APPROACH: From the highway, set off upwards on the east (climber's right) side of the creek.

Travel beside the creek can be quite arduous near the valley bottom. Trend slightly climber's right while fighting bush, aiming for a rock-filled clearing at around 1700 metres elevation (GR 641759). Once you are in the clearing, travel becomes much less arduous. Carry on for another 400 vertical metres to the start of the broad summit plateau. Head north to the western edge of the summit ridge amidst undulating small hills. Once on the ridge, head east and follow the ridgecrest to a large, cairned high point. If you have extra energy it is easily possible to carry on eastwards along the ridge to several more high points on the way to Razor Peak.

The "Kain's Ridge" ascent route viewed from above, near treeline. Taking the large, rubbly avalanche path pictured at centre right reduces bushwhacking.

There is quite a large cairn at the high point along the ridge. Mount Kain can be seen in the background.

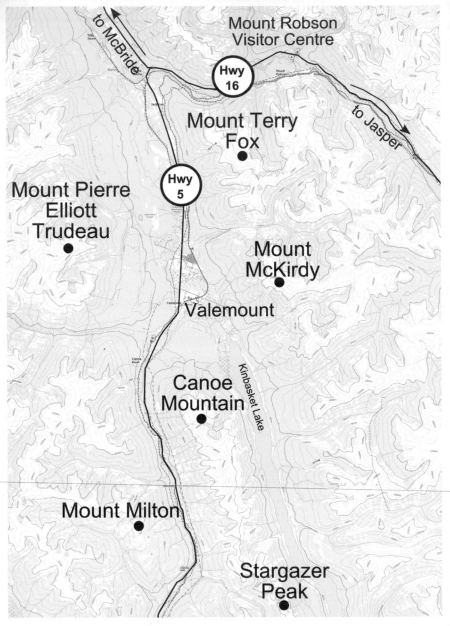

Mount Robson
Visitor Centre

to McBride

Hwy
16

to Jasper

Mount Terry
Fox

Hwy
5

Mount Pierre
Elliott
Trudeau

Mount
McKirdy

Valemount

Canoe
Mountain

Kinbasket Lake

Mount Milton

Stargazer
Peak

# VALEMOUNT

| MOUNTAIN | ELEVATION (M) | ROUTE TYPE | PAGE |
|----------|---------------|------------|------|
| Canoe Mountain | 2654 | On-trail hike | 266 |
| Mount McKirdy | 2592 | Moderate scramble | 268 |
| Mount Milton | 2135 | Easy scramble | 270 |
| Mount Pierre Elliott Trudeau | 2637 | Alpine climb (5.3) | 272 |
| Mount Terry Fox | 2651 | On-trail hike | 274 |
| Stargazer Peak | 2404 | Easy scramble | 276 |

## AREA OVERVIEW

Nestled west of Mount Robson Provincial Park lies the village of Valemount, a unique municipality which borders three different mountain ranges: the Rockies, the Cariboos, and the Monashees (the latter two being part of the Columbia Mountains of the BC Interior Range; four routes are included from this range, as they are excellent viewpoints looking back into the Rockies). This fact is celebrated in the name of a microbrewery in town (Three Ranges Brewing Company). For peakbaggers the Valemount region offers numerous opportunities and challenges and a break from some of the common scenery in more familiar areas.

## ACCESS, ACCOMMODATIONS AND FACILITIES

Valemount can be accessed via Hwy 16, from Jasper in the east or McBride to the northwest, or by way of Hwy 5 from Kamloops to the south.

There are numerous places to stay in the area, including several hotels and an assortment of frontcountry lodges and campsites. Check with the Valemount visitor centre or visit valemount.ca for an up-to-date list.

Some food and supplies can be obtained in Valemount, with a wider selection possible by journeying eastwards to Jasper.

## PERMITS AND RESTRICTIONS

There are far fewer restrictions than in the national parks, but check with the Valemount visitor centre (785 Cranberry Lake Road, just off the highway at the intersection with 5th Avenue) for any recent area closures or trail restrictions. Be aware that quadding (summer) and sledding (winter) are very popular activities in the region, and many of the hiking approach trails are shared between mechanized and more traditional travellers.

Kinbasket Lake is an exceptionally long geographic feature stretching from Valemount in the north to near Golden in the south.

Mechanized tourism is exceedingly popular in Valemount as these sled-tracked slopes near Mount Milton do attest.

## CANOE MOUNTAIN, 2654 M ☐

Difficulty:
on-trail hike (2nd, F)

Hazards:
ATVs or snowmobiles

Round-trip distance:
25 km

Total elevation gain:
1900 m

Round-trip time:
10–13 hours

Recommended seasons:
summer; fall; winter (skis)

ATES rating:
challenging

Map:
83D11 Canoe Mountain

*At the northernmost tip of the Monashee Range, the oddly named Canoe Mountain was named for the Canoe River, which in turn was named by David Thompson. The shape of the Canoe River was drastically altered starting in 1973 due to the completion of Mica Dam and the consequent formation of Kinbasket Lake.*

ACCESS: From the shoulder of Hwy 5 at 15.2 km south of Valemount. Park near a metal shed on the east side of the road.

APPROACH: The route starts directly from the roadside.

The route follows a clear-cut which serves as an ATV/snowmobile road. Views are quite

Looking across the valley from the summit of Mount Milton to Canoe Mountain (C). Mount Robson (R) looms in the distance.

Looking back down the ascent route from above treeline on Canoe Mountain. Photo: Steven Song.

limited until you reach treeline (8.2 km and 1250 metres of elevation from the trailhead). The "trail" is broad and can be easily followed as it winds upwards. At treeline there is still a little over 4 km of distance and 600 metres of elevation to the summit. Near the summit, as is common in BC, there is a large weather station to check out, though your eyes will almost certainly be drawn to the excellent views of Mount Robson and countless peaks down Kinbasket Lake. This is a popular route for ATVs in summer and snowmobiles in winter, so keep your eyes and ears open to avoid any collisions!

## MOUNT McKIRDY VIA CARSON'S PEAK, 2592 M □

Difficulty:
moderate scramble (3rd, F)

Hazards:
rockfall; early-season
avalanches

Round-trip distance:
17 km

Total elevation gain:
1700 m

Round-trip time:
9–11 hours

Recommended seasons:
summer; fall

Map:
83D14 Valemount

*Fulton Alexander McKirdy was a pioneer in the Valemount region, and there are several ways to access his mountain. The route described here is a scenic highline traverse over a ridge known locally as "Carson's Peak."*

ACCESS: Head east on 5th Avenue in Valemount until the street ends in a T intersection with Main Street. Then turn right (south) for barely 150 m before taking a left (east) up Hillside Road. Follow the sign on the left for Swift Mountain Forest Road (also known as 5 Mile Road) and drive upwards.

It is 6.5 km and 700 m of elevation to a parking area at around 1500 m. In winter, self-propelled trips will likely start at the bottom of the forest road, making for some additional exercise!

The route up Carson's Peak (C) and Mount McKirdy (M) as seen from across the valley. Photo: Eric Coulthard.

VALEMOUNT MOUNT McKIRDY VIA CARSON'S PEAK

At the summit of Carson's Peak with Mount McKirdy in the background.

APPROACH: From the parking lot the trail is marked with an old BC Forest Service sign stating "3 MILES TO THE ALPINE." Follow the trail as it steeply winds upwards.

After 3 km the elevation gain lets up and you reach the first alpine meadow. A sign points left toward the YORA (Yellowhead Outdoor Recreation Association) cabin. (If you would like to stay overnight in the cabin, check with the visitor centre ahead of time.) The route to Mount McKirdy follows a trail which becomes faint but is extensively flagged. If you do lose your way, trend almost due east, aiming for a ridge across a meadow which connects up to "Carson's Peak." Stick near the ridgecrest to the cairned summit of Carson's Peak at an elevation of 2400 m. From the summit, carry on along the ridge, dropping down to the west side as you descend towards the Carson's/McKirdy col. Ascend Mount McKirdy via its northwest ridge on a combination of scree and boulders that yields to dinner-plate style rock near the summit. Return the way you came.

Difficulty: easy scramble
(2nd, F)

Hazards:
snowmobiles; early-season
avalanches

Round-trip distance:
28 km

Total elevation gain:
1800 m

Round-trip time:
10–12 hours

Recommended seasons:
summer; fall; winter (skis)

ATES rating:
challenging

Map:
83D11 Canoe Mountain

*This is another peak named by Dr. W.B. Cheadle after his travelling companion William Wentworth Fitzwilliam (whose name also graces Mount Fitzwilliam along the Yellowhead Highway). Fitzwilliam also held the title Viscount Milton. The slopes around Mount Milton are best known to snowmobilers as the Allan Creek sledding area.*

ACCESS: Via Hwy 5, 35 km south of Valemount. The parking area is on the west side of the road (and is widely plowed in the winter to accommodate snowmobile trailers).

APPROACH: From the trailhead, there is an 8 km road that leads upwards into the alpine and ends at the Allan Creek cabin (1100 vertical metres from the trailhead).

North from the summit of Mount Milton, with the Premier Range at centre left and Valemount village in the valley to the right.

At the Allan Creek cabin looking towards the rest of the route up Mount Milton.
Photo: Steven Song

In winter this road sees a great deal of traffic – so much, in fact, that it is gated and a trail-grooming fee is charged for snowmobile access. It is a good idea to check in with the folks at the gate to let sledders know there are people on foot around!

The route up Mount Milton first follows the snowmobile road to the cabin and then carries on northwards. A little over 1 km from the cabin, descend down gentle, treed slopes onto a plateau that carries on northwest towards Mount Milton. A few minor bumps are overcome or traversed before the final slope is reached that grants access to the broad summit. Views of Mount Robson to the northeast and Mount Albreda to the southeast make this a worthwhile ascent. If you have extra energy it is easily possible to keep exploring the alpine terrain by heading west along the ridge from the summit to several unnamed peaks (though with significant elevation loss). When you've had your fill of views, ramble back the way you came. In winter, descent down the approach road can be particularly swift on skis. Watch out for snowmobiles!

Difficulty:
alpine climb (5.3, PD−)

Hazards:
rockfall; early-season
avalanches

Round-trip distance:
10.5 km

Total elevation gain:
1400 m

Round-trip time:
11–13 hours

Recommended seasons:
summer; fall

Map:
83D14 Valemount

*Pierre Elliott Trudeau, Canada's 15th prime minister, was a widely popular politician from the 1960s into the 1980s. There was great controversy in 2000 when, after Trudeau's death, Prime Minister Jean Chrétien sought to rename Canada's highest peak (Mount Logan) as "Mount Trudeau." The proposal was thoroughly disdained by the mountain community and the public at large, and this peak was chosen to bear Trudeau's name as a compromise.*

<u>*Note*</u> *that there's a proposed plan for a new ski resort at Valemount which would turn this terrain into part of the resort and likely change much of the route described here.*

Looking up toward Mount Pierre Elliott Trudeau (T). The red ascent line winds up the east ridge, occasionally veering onto the face. The alternative descent line in green is especially quick if snow conditions are amenable to glissading.
Photo: Eric Coulthard.

. ACCESS: Via Cariboo Lodge Road, accessed from Hwy 5 at 3 km south of Valemount. Turn right onto Cariboo Lodge Road and drive until you reach the signed West Ridge Forest Road. The trailhead parking lot is 15 km from the highway and is marked with a BC Forest Service sign. The trailhead is at 1325 m and GR 392564. A four-wheel drive vehicle is useful for the road, particularly if there has been recent rainfall.

APPROACH: From the trailhead, set off on the (slightly overgrown) trail. After just over 1 km the trail crosses a creek that flows down from Mount Trudeau and is unbridged (though there are downed trees nearby to help). Once past the creek, the trail stays fairly low in the valley through marshy terrain until it reaches the lower of two alpine bowls and a small meltwater pond. The ascent and descent routes diverge from this point.

To ascend the east ridge, gain 200 vertical metres on grassy rubble while trending climber's left (south) to a wide plateau above the second alpine bowl. This plateau marks the start of the east ridge. Ascend the ridge to a high point at 2350 metres. From the high point, lose a small amount of elevation, staying near the crest of the ridge before reaching rockbands. From here the route stays near the crest of the ridge, trending slightly climber's right and working steadily upwards. Expect consistent 4th class terrain with several individual moves up to 5.3 which can be minimized with route-finding. You can bypass some of the exposed sections by moving slightly onto the east face, particularly in the early season when lingering snow patches allow for solid footholds. Some 100 metres below the summit, trend climber's right on difficult scrambling terrain to intersect with the north ridge. Once on the north ridge, follow it on moderate rock to reach additional difficult scrambling terrain on the very exposed summit block. On descent, follow the north ridge, losing 200 vertical metres before reaching the top of a large snow/scree slope on the northwest face. Following this slope, continue downwards, trending gradually skier's left (north) to reach the higher alpine bowl and a trio of tarns. To return to the approach trail, head farther north to grassy rubble slopes which lead downwards to the first alpine bowl and back to the trailhead.

**Difficulty:**
on-trail hike (2nd, F)

**Hazards:**
few

**Round-trip distance:**
23 km

**Total elevation gain:**
1850 m

**Round-trip time:**
11–13 hours

**Recommended seasons:**
summer; fall

**Map:**
83D14 Valemount

*Terry Fox became famous for his "Marathon of Hope," a trans-Canada trek on foot to raise funds for cancer research. A cancer sufferer himself, Terry eventually succumbed to the disease after it forced him to stop his marathon near Thunder Bay, Ontario, in 1980. In 1981 this mountain was named after him, and later in 1981 the area surrounding the peak was made into a new provincial park also commemorating Terry Fox.*

ACCESS: The trailhead can be reached just north of Valemount by turning right onto Stone Road (directly across from the signed Terry Fox Rest Area). Immediately after reaching Stone Road, turn left onto Tinsley Road and cross a set of railway tracks to follow a rough road up to the trailhead. There are several signed private roads along the way, so be sure to stay on the main road to avoid trespassing.

The trail up Mount Terry Fox snakes upwards (not all of the switchbacks are drawn here) before emerging into the alpine and sticking near the ridgecrest onwards to the summit.

APPROACH: The trail starts directly from the parking lot. Remember to bring plenty of water for this route.

The Mount Terry Fox trail winds upwards with an impressive 17 switchbacks (thankfully, some are very short) before flattening out into the alpine. The route has a number of viewpoints looking west across the valley towards peaks of the Premier Range. Once you reach treeline (around 1000 vertical metres from trailhead) the track can become harder to follow but there are numerous cairns to aid navigation. The trail leads to a prominent false summit (complete with radio repeater) at an elevation of 2480 m before traversing above four alpine lakes and following the crest of a ridge to the summit. Just before the summit, be careful to stay on the ridge and not wander onto the glaciated northwest face. On descent, if you have extra energy, it is worthwhile to explore the alpine lakes accessible from the low point of the trail running below the false summit.

The alpine lakes and in the distance Mount Robson from the upper part of the Mount Terry Fox trail. Photo: Eric Coulthard.

Difficulty:
easy scramble (2nd, F)

Hazards:
snowmobiles; early-season avalanches

Round-trip distance:
15 km
(from 1250 m parking)

Total elevation gain:
1200 m
(from 1250 m parking)

Round-trip time:
7–10 hours
(from 1250 m parking)

Recommended season:
fall, winter (snowshoes)

ATES rating:
challenging

Maps:
83D11 Canoe Mountain;
83D10 Ptarmigan Creek

*An unofficially named peak above the west shore of Kinbasket Lake. As a viewpoint this would be a fabulous place for stargazing. Thankfully the views during the day are quite nice as well (especially looking south towards Mount Albreda)!*

ACCESS: Via the Clemina Creek FSR, 30 km south of Valemount on Hwy 5 (the signed trailhead is on the east side of the road). If the FSR is not snow-covered, it may be possible to drive farther along it to shorten the approach hike (be careful to park somewhere that does not block ATV traffic). In winter (generally starting in late November), the road becomes the groomed access route to the Clemina Creek sledding area, and highway vehicle travel is restricted past the side of the highway. There is a good parking area at 9 km and another at the Clemina Creek cabin 17 km down the road. The route described here starts at the 9 km parking area (at an elevation of 1250 m and GR 622266).

APPROACH: Snowshoe or hike 4 km along the FSR as it heads toward the base of Stargazer Peak, until you reach the signed "Morning Glory" snowmobile track starting on climber's left (north).

From the start of the "Morning Glory" track, wend your way first to the northeast before settling out due eastward, leaving the snowmobile trail and making a beeline for the alpine. After leaving the FSR, there

Snowshoeing up the approach road. The route starting at the "Morning Glory" snowmobile trail is shown leading to the summit (S). Photo: Steven Song.

is 2 km of distance and 400 metres of elevation to be dispatched before breaking out of the trees. Route-finding options are plentiful, with gentler terrain reached by staying farther south near a creek flowing from nearby Goat Ridge. A more direct line heads northeast through steep forested slopes (well suited for snowshoes in winter), ending up at the base of the final slope to the summit of Stargazer. Whichever route you choose, ascend the peak by its south face, gaining 300 vertical metres before reaching the summit weather tower. On descent, a worthwhile extension can be to explore the alpine meadows beneath the peak, especially in summer when the nearby lake offers a nice place for lunch.

# BIBLIOGRAPHY

The following sources were referenced in preparing this book. Additional information was obtained from personal records of the authors.

## BOOKS

Boles, Glen, Roger Laurilla and William L. Putnam. *Canadian Mountain Place Names*. Calgary: Rocky Mountain Books, 2006. Originally published as *Place Names of the Canadian Alps*, Revelstoke, BC: Footprint, c1990.

Corbett, Bill. *The 11000ers of the Canadian Rockies*. 2nd ed. Calgary: Rocky Mountain Books, 2016.

Eng, Ronald C., and Julie Van Pelt. *Mountaineering: The Freedom of the Hills*. 8th ed. Seattle: The Mountaineers Books, 2010.

Gadd, Ben. *Handbook of the Canadian Rockies*. 2nd ed. Jasper, Alta.: Corax Press, 1995.

Kane, Alan. *Scrambles in the Canadian Rockies*. 3rd ed. Calgary: Rocky Mountain Books, 2016.

Patton, Brian, and Bart Robinson. *The Canadian Rockies Trail Guide*. 9th ed. Banff: Summerthought Publishing, 2011.

Tilton, Buck. *Wilderness First Responder*. 3rd ed. Guilford, Conn.: Morris Book Publishing/Falcon Guides, 2010.

## WEBSITES

Alberta Parks. "Whitehorse Wildland Provincial Park." Accessed 2016-09-16 at albertaparks.ca/whitehorse.aspx.

Association of Canadian Mountain Guides (ACMG). "Public Mountain Conditions Reports." Excellent descriptions of current conditions across the Rockies from accredited guides. Accessed 2016-09-16 at mountainconditions.com.

Avalanche Canada. Avalanche hazard reports and mountain weather forecasts for the Canadian Rockies as well as the BC Interior and Coast Ranges. Accessed 2016-09-16 at avalanche.ca.

BC Parks. "Mount Robson Provincial Park." Accessed 2016-09-16 at www.env.gov.bc.ca/bcparks/explore/parkpgs/mt_robson.

Coulthard, Eric. "Summit Search Mountain Community." A personal website with an encyclopedic compendium of mountain imagery and route information. Accessed 2016-09-16 at www.summitsearch.org.

Dewit, Vern. "explor8ion." A personal website containing well-described information on hikes, scrambles and alpine routes across the Canadian Rockies. Accessed 2016-09-16 at explor8ion.com.

Google Earth. An excellent tool for combining digitally obtained elevation data with satellite imagery to plot possible routelines. Accessed 2016-09-16 at google.com/earth.

Nearingburg, Ben. "Ben's Hikes, Scrambles and Mountaineering Trips." A personal website with numerous trip reports and mountain photos from Canadian peaks and beyond. Accessed 2016-09-16 at benthereclimbedthat.ca.

Parks Canada. "Jasper National Park." Accessed 2016-09-16 at pc.gc.ca/eng/pn-np/ab/jasper/index.aspx.

Song, Steven. "Steven's Peak-Bagging Journey." A personal website comprised of trip reports for the Canadian Rockies and the British Columbia Interior and Coast Ranges. Accessed 2016-09-16 at stevensong.com.

SpotWx. An exceptionally useful multi-source weather service for accurate forecasts keyed to your specific location. Accessed 2016-09-16 at spotwx.com.

# USEFUL CONTACTS

**For Yellowhead Highway East and West, Maligne Lake, Tonquin Valley, Icefields Parkway, Le Grand Brazeau, South Boundary Trail and Whitehorse Wildland Provincial Park:**

Ambulance/police/fire: 911

Park wardens (24 hours for emergencies): 780-852-6155

Information centre: 780-852-6176

Backcountry-trail reservations: 1-877-RESERVE (1-877-737-3783);

pc.gc.ca/bookjasperbackcountry

**For Whitehorse Wildland Provincial Park, add:**

Whitehorse Wildland Information: 780-865-8395

**For Mount Robson Provincial Park:**

Ambulance/police/fire: 911

Mount Robson Visitor Centre: 250-566-4038

**For Valemount:**

Ambulance/police/fire: 911

Valemount Visitor Centre: 250-566-9893,

visitvalemount.ca/plan/visitor-centre

# TABLE OF WINTER PEAKS

Winter can often be a challenging time for the peakbagger to choose suitable objectives. The following summits have routes that are good trips to do over the long Canadian winter, whether on skis or snowshoes (see each respective peak entry for a recommendation). Be sure to check the described avalanche terrain ratings, take appropriate precautions and ensure you have complete safety equipment before setting off on any winter trip (or spring trip in the main ranges, which can hold on to the chill of winter well into the start of "summer" as felt in the front ranges).

| | | |
|---|---|---|
| ☐ Aberhart, Mount | 117 | ☐ McDonell Peak | 150 |
| ☐ Amber Mountain | 120 | ☐ Miette Pass Peaks | 99 |
| ☐ Anne-Alice, Mount | 250 | ☐ Milton, Mount | 270 |
| ☐ Campion Mountain | 242 | ☐ Oliver, Mount | 90 |
| ☐ Canoe Mountain | 266 | ☐ Palisade, The | 86 |
| ☐ "Chilly Peak" | 178 | ☐ Pattison, Mount | 92 |
| ☐ Cinquefoil Mountain | 36 | ☐ Simon Peak | 148 |
| ☐ Elysium Mountain | 88 | ☐ Sirdar Mountain | 110 |
| ☐ Evelyn Peak | 164 | ☐ Stargazer Peak | 276 |
| ☐ Folding Mountain | 38 | ☐ Sunset Peak | 116 |
| ☐ Ghita Mountain | 258 | ☐ Sunwapta Peak | 172 |
| ☐ Hardisty, Mount | 166 | ☐ Thunderbolt Peak | 146 |
| ☐ Maccarib, Mount | 142 | ☐ "Verdant Hill" | 152 |

# INDEX OF ALL PEAKS AND ROUTES

☐ Aberhart, Mount, 117

☐ Amber Mountain, 120

☐ Anne-Alice, Mount, 250

☐ Bald Hills, 106

☐ Bedson Ridge, 28

☐ "Bivy Ridge," 212

☐ Black Cat Mountain, 34

☐ Boule Roche, 30

☐ Brazeau, Mount, 202

☐ Bucephalus Peak, 254

☐ Cairngorm, 82

☐ Campion Mountain, 242

☐ Canoe Mountain, 266

☐ Cardinal Divide Ridge, 226

☐ Catacombs Mountain, 158

☐ Centre Mountain, 122

☐ Chetamon Mountain, 56

☐ Cheviot Mountain, 230

☐ "Chilly Peak," 178

☐ Cinnamon Peak, 238

☐ Cinquefoil Mountain, 36

☐ "Claw, The," 180

☐ Clitheroe, Mount, 138

☐ Coronet Mountain, 200

☐ Cumnock, Mount, 60

☐ Curator Mountain, 119

☐ Diadem Peak, 186

☐ Edith Cavell, Mount, 140

☐ Elysium Mountain, 88

☐ Esplanade Mountain, 62

☐ Evelyn Peak, 164

☐ Excelsior Mountain, 123

☐ Fitzwilliam, Mount, 252

☐ Folding Mountain, 38

☐ Fortress Mountain, 162

☐ Fryatt, Mount, 170

☐ Gargoyle Mountain, 64

☐ Geraldine Peak, 168

☐ Ghita Mountain, 258

☐ GMMC Mountain, 224

☐ Hardisty, Mount, 166

☐ Hawk Mountain, 40

☐ Henry MacLeod, Mount, 206

☐ Henry, Mount, 84

☐ Indian Peak, 96

☐ "Kain's Ridge," 260

☐ Kerr, Mount, 83

☐ Little Alberta, 192

☐ Maccarib, Mount, 142

☐ McDonell Peak, 150

☐ McKirdy, Mount, 268

☐ Memorial Peak, 144

☐ Miette Pass Peaks, 99

☐ Milton, Mount, 270

☐ Morro Peak, 42

☐ Muhigan Mountain, 98

☐ Mumm Peak, 246

☐ Mushroom Peak, 190

☐ O'Hagan, Mount, 44

☐ Oliver, Mount, 90

☐ Opal Peak, 108
☐ Palisade, The, 86
☐ Pattison, Mount, 92
☐ Pierre Elliott Trudeau, Mount, 272
☐ Poboktan Mountain, 214
☐ Pyramid Mountain, 80
☐ "Rabbit Ears," 46
☐ Redan Mountain, 66
☐ Replica Peak, 216
☐ Roche à Perdrix, 48
☐ Roche Bonhomme, 112
☐ Roche de Smet, 68
☐ Roche Miette, 50
☐ Signal Mountain, 128
☐ Simon Peak, 148
☐ Sirdar Mountain, 110
☐ Skyline Trail, 114
☐ Southern Victoria Cross Range
  Traverse, 74
☐ Southesk Cairn, 222
☐ Stargazer Peak, 276
☐ Sunset Peak, 116
☐ Sunwapta Peak (North Glacier), 172
☐ Sunwapta Peak (Southwest Face), 174
☐ Tangle Ridge, 176
☐ Tekarra, Mount, 126
☐ Terry Fox, Mount, 274
☐ Thunderbolt Peak, 146
☐ Titkana Peak, 244
☐ Tripoli Mountain, 228

☐ Utopia Mountain, 52
☐ Valad Peak, 208
☐ "Verdant Hill," 152
☐ Warren, Mount, 210
☐ Wentworth, Mount, 256
☐ Whistlers, The, 94
☐ Woolley, Mount, 182

**Ben Nearingburg** is a research scientist/instructor by day, but at most other times he roams the hills of the Canadian Rockies and Columbia ranges. Coming from a background of distance hiking and indoor climbing, Ben has been drawn to the triad of good exercise, fabulous views and great company that mountainous pursuits provide. In 2016 Ben started down the road of becoming a certified hiking guide, to share his passion of the mountains both on and off the written page. He lives in Edmonton, Alberta.

**Eric Coulthard** is a computer scientist. He is the founder and developer of summitsearch.org, a mountain community site with an encyclopedia, trip reports, a forum and over 15,000 mountain photos. When it comes to mountain trips, Eric loves exploring. Many of his top treks are exploratory jaunts with little or no beta. The ability to draw routes and use the photos on summitsearch.org helps immensely in planning his explorations. One of Eric's goals is to get a photo of every named peak in the Canadian Rockies onto summitsearch.org. He also hopes to visit every icefield in the Rockies. Outside of work and mountains, Eric is a devoted husband and father. He lives in Edmonton, Alberta.